Philosophy as a Guide to Living
Part I

Professor Stephen A. Erickson

THE TEACHING COMPANY ®

PUBLISHED BY:

THE TEACHING COMPANY
4151 Lafayette Center Drive, Suite 100
Chantilly, Virginia 20151-1232
1-800-TEACH-12
Fax—703-378-3819
www.teach12.com

ISBN 1-59803-138-4

Stephen A. Erickson, Ph.D.
Professor of Philosophy, Pomona College

Steve Erickson received his Ph.D. in philosophy from Yale University at the age of 23. Since 1964, he has taught philosophy at Pomona College, where he is a professor of philosophy and holds the E. Wilson Lyon Chair in the Humanities. He is the author of *Language and Being* (Yale University Press), *Human Presence: At the Boundaries of Meaning* (Mercer University Press), and *The (Coming) Age of Thresholding* (Kluwer Academic Publishers), as well as numerous articles published in such journals as *The Review of Metaphysics, Man and World, Philosophy Today, The Harvard Review of Philosophy*, and the *International Philosophical Quarterly*.

Professor Erickson has been a guest faculty member at a number of psychoanalytic institutes, including the Los Angeles Psychoanalytic Institute and the Institute for Contemporary Psychoanalysis, and has been a visiting scholar in New Hall, Cambridge University, Cambridge, England, and the University of Groningen in the Netherlands. He has served as president of the Karl Jaspers Society of North America and was a member of the Planning Committee for the Millennium Conference on Integration in the United Kingdom. He has recently served on the American Philosophical Association (APA) Committee on the Status and Future of the Profession and has been a director of conferences for the Liberty Fund, Inc., Indianapolis, Indiana, for more than 20 years. He is a member of the International Advisory Board of the Centre for Fundamental Research in Modern Culture, St. Petersburg, Russia; serves as the chair of the Academic Advisory Board of *Collegium Hieronymi Pragensis* in Prague, Czech Republic; and serves on the Editorial Advisory Board of the *Journal of Medicine and Philosophy* in the United States.

Professor Erickson has received awards from the National Endowment for the Humanities, the American Council of Learned Societies, and the Earhart Foundation, as well as four Wig Awards at Pomona College for excellence in teaching. He has lectured throughout the United States and Europe and in South America and Asia and currently leads conferences and seminars that deal with our controversially globalized transition into the 21st century, the promise of human freedom, and the spiritual and cultural challenges we face.

Table of Contents
Philosophy as a Guide to Living
Part I

Professor Biography i
Course Scope 1
Lecture One   The Axial Model 5
Lecture Two   Kant's Hopeful Program 21
Lecture Three   The Kantian Legacy 34
Lecture Four   Kant and the Romantic Reaction 48
Lecture Five   Hegel on the Human Spirit 63
Lecture Six   Hegel on State and Society 78
Lecture Seven   Hegel on Selfhood and Human Identity........... 92
Lecture Eight   Schopenhauer's Pessimism 105
Lecture Nine   Schopenhauer's Remedies 119
Lecture Ten   Alienation in Marx 132
Lecture Eleven   Marx's Utopian Hope 146
Lecture Twelve   Kierkegaard's Crises 160
Timeline 174
Glossary 178
Biographical Notes 188
Bibliography 194

Philosophy as a Guide to Living

Scope:

Is there a meaning to human life? Can this question be answered by philosophy? If so, could any positive answer be pursued through the practice of philosophy itself?

These questions became increasingly timely, haunting, and controversial among European philosophers after the Enlightenment (c. 1750) when reason came more and more to trump religion as a way of explaining the world and our place in it. These questions remain timely and controversial today. They are the focus of *Philosophy as a Guide to Living* and are considered through the lenses of mostly European (Continental) philosophers, who have reflected on them from the time of the Enlightenment to the present.

Why single out these philosophers in particular? Because they speak in important ways to the time in which we now find ourselves. They are concerned with exploring the limits of human reason and are focused on the likely course of history. These philosophers tend also to pay close attention to our lives *in* the world, enmeshed in culture and questing after significant opportunities for self-understanding and personal development.

Though we are *in*, we are not altogether *of* this world, even if, in no literal sense, any other world exists.

This statement captures what I will be referring to as the *axial sensibility*: the sense that we find ourselves caught up largely in *appearances* and are trapped in and subject to various forms of bondage, such as political, psychological, and possibly spiritual ones. Coupled with this sense is the further sense that there must be an *elsewhere*, or another and better way of being here in the world as it is now, one that better engages *reality* and gives us a sense of liberation rather than confinement. This *axial* sense may prove to be but an inchoate and unrealistic longing, but it has been and continues to be experienced by many as genuine and inescapable. It has often been described as a *longing for a belonging*, driven in part by a sense of not belonging to the world as it is, of being displaced in it.

The claim became a focus and battleground for philosophers after the Enlightenment, and our course will continually return to its differing and often conflicting meanings. Thus, this course will be as much in depth as in extension. It will take no position but will probe and explore many. It will do this primarily through the telling of a philosophical story that has unfolded over the last 250 years and continues to inform our present.

A central dimension of this story is ancient, however. It needs to be kept in mind as our adventure unfolds. As I have indicated, the philosophical and religious West has been *axial*. It has understood human life as a journey: from appearance to reality, bondage to liberation, confusion to insight, darkness to light, the changing to the unchanging, and time to eternity. Until the time of the Enlightenment the task of life was largely construed as overcoming ignorance and bondage through direct and transforming encounter with reality. But this *axial* vision suffered a major blow from within philosophy itself. It is with this blow that our story really begins.

The German philosopher Immanuel Kant (1724–1804), whose ideas are considered by many to represent a great watershed in Western thought, based all human hope on reason alone, dismissing all alternatives as forms of superstition. Yet he also claimed that our reason was limited in its scope and that our true humanity was available to us only if we considered certain fundamental metaphysical questions, even though the answers to these questions would be inaccessible to our rational capacities. Here already a disturbing paradox is found in Kant's writing, and intense controversy soon erupted. If reason—perhaps best exhibited today as technology—is our indispensable ally, and Kant himself claims that it must fail us in the end, how could knowledge of ultimate matters be possible? What could possibly serve as a foundation for human hope? In differing ways, all the philosophers we will consider in this course take up the challenge of answering these questions.

Beyond these questions lie even more. If, finally, reason cannot be relied upon, and religion, supposedly, has been superseded by Enlightenment thinking, by what means can claims about human extraordinariness be sustained? Did not the notion of a "metaphysical dimension to the human" become simply another superstition to overcome? In varying ways, the philosophers whom we consider in this course take up the challenge of responding to these questions as well.

Part of philosophy's post–Enlightenment quest for meaning involves attempts at finding something more fundamental in human beings than reason and a goal more elemental and transforming than knowledge. The truth, it has been said, will set people free. This notion is at the core of the *axial* understanding of human life. But perhaps there is no truth, just facts. And perhaps no wisdom, either, just information.

Could it be that liberation, not knowledge, is the true end purpose of human life and even its meaning? And might this liberation be achieved through nonrational means: power, sexuality, revolution, resignation, creativity, compassion, or solidarity? All these pathways are explored in differing ways by Continental philosophers such as Nietzsche, Freud, Marx, Schopenhauer, Heidegger, Foucault, and others—all seeking a meaning to human life through a diagnosis of what the supposed "predicament of human existence" actually is. All assume that there *is* a human predicament, that it can be understood, and that it can, to some significant degree, be surmounted. What, in fact, *is* the human predicament? If this predicament is not so much ignorance (of something) as bondage (to something), what must we be liberated *from,* and what are we thereby liberated *for*? Liberation that is merely *from* something has a problematic, negative possibility accompanying it. Once liberated, we humans might find nothing positive in relation to which to exercise our newly acquired freedom. The resulting danger is something that has been called *nihilism*, the "discovery" that nowhere is to be found anything deserving our devotion or support, *that life has no meaning.*

Nihilism is in fact a genuine danger and concern for many of the philosophers whom we will consider in this course, including Schopenhauer, Nietzsche, and Heidegger. We will be taking a close look at nihilism, its motivations, dynamics, and conflicting strands. Is nihilism avoidable and, in any case, can it be overcome by philosophical means? Does philosophy have resources to guide us around or through and beyond nihilism? The French Existentialist John Paul Sartre says that meaningful life begins on the other side of despair. What sense might we make of such a claim?

Many say that the 21st century is a *postmodern age,* and that postmodernism is inherently nihilistic. Postmodernism is said by some to close the door on all sustainable quests for meaning and even to render philosophy itself obsolete. In the light of our preceding explorations, I will suggest alternative ways in which philosophy may nonetheless thrive in our time, pursuing the quest for meaning and thereby providing various *guides to living.*

Lecture One
The Axial Model

Scope:

The philosophical and religious understanding of life in the West has been *axial* for almost 3,000 years, emerging with the Ancients. We will explore how axial thinking, the understanding of life as a journey, came into being and how it has shaped our belief systems. During the *Enlightenment*, the axial vision suffered a major blow from within philosophy itself. The German philosopher Immanuel Kant, whose ideas are considered by many to represent a great watershed in Western thought, based all human hope on reason alone, dismissing alternatives as forms of superstition. Professional philosophy taught in our colleges and universities today still takes its impetus primarily from Enlightenment thinking. We will explore the major philosophical trends, from Kant through modernity, that have influenced and shaped the way that we perceive the world today. Our journey will be a somewhat unusual one. It will be a narrative overview of particular philosophical perspectives, but it will also be a consideration of where we are in point and time on the axial path and how to perceive the future of the human spirit.

Outline

I. Over the course of this series of lectures, I will be taking you on a journey. It will be an unusual journey in certain respects, and I want to outline its contours and some of its uncommon features before we begin.

   A. We will be looking at whether or not there may be a deeper meaning to human life than we ordinarily experience and whether or not philosophy can help us to determine what that meaning might be.

      1. Some might say that such matters come down to whether we are healthy or not, whether we enjoy life or not, and whether or not we are successful.

      2. Others might feel that such matters are private and belong to the realm of religion.

      3. During our journey together, we will respect both of these viewpoints but will follow a philosophical path

B. There are three fundamental questions that we must ask within the context of philosophy:

   1. Is reliable knowledge of our human nature possible? In fact, do human beings even have a nature?

   2. In a time such as ours, perhaps far less superstitious than disenchanted, what might be the human predicament?

   3. Can human life be lived with both integrity and fulfillment?

C. Some of the issues that we will discuss together are complicated and controversial, but I'll hope to present a number of perspectives with which to engage you. No one could agree with all of them.

   1. If you agree with some of these views as we go along, then I hope you will value them and be enriched by them.

   2. If you disagree with them, I hope that you will dwell on them nonetheless, if only to stimulate your thinking even further.

II. Let us look for a moment at the backdrop from which the sorts of ideas we will be considering arose.

A. We start with an ancient model, the axial model, which was developed somewhere between 800–200 B.C.E. In the axial model, a sharp distinction was made between this world and a world beyond, and the idea arose that, although we are *in* this world, we are not *of* this world. According to this model, human life is a journey that leads from appearance to reality, bondage to liberation, confusion to insight, and darkness to light.

B. In the 18th century, the Enlightenment challenged this axial notion. It was thought important to abandon the past and all old beliefs and superstitions and move on to a determination that our own human reason is the instrument through which our lives find their paths to meaning.

III. We will be looking more at "big pictures" as we continue, rather than focusing on narrow, specifically defined problems.

A. For example, we will look at what human beings in past centuries were concerned about.

1. In the ancient world, the great human concern was with death—how the fact that we die affects us and how it forces us to understand life.

2. We will note a time, often associated with the Protestant Reformation, when the overarching human concern was with guilt: Are we doing the right thing? What ought we do? Why do we not always do the right thing?

3. In our time, and especially from the 20th century on, we arrive at a concern with meaning. It is not a question of rightness or wrongness but, rather, what is it that really matters? Is there anything worth doing? Is there anything that is genuinely meaningful?

B. Another big picture suggests that if you start with the philosophy of Plato—a great believer that we are not of this world and a philosopher who distinguished between appearance and reality—the relentless development of Western thought brings us eventually to a world today where technology triumphs. This world is one where technology is viewed more and more as the solution to everything and where human life, therefore, is altogether in this world and does not have a home elsewhere.

C. A third view leads to Nietzsche. He says that Western thought has developed in such a way that sources of significant experience are dwindling. Therefore, fewer and fewer things matter—in short, that meaning in a deeper sense no longer has any grounding.

IV. Ours is an uncertain time, when everything is questioned. We are concerned about politics, economics, and natural disasters. We see controversies about the nature and future of religion. Underlying these worries is the desire to have an overview that makes sense of all these issues.

A. When the axial model was in place, people understood themselves on a journey in life.

B. With the Enlightenment, reason came to replace faith and tradition.

C. Do we live in a world now where we have no overview, no schema to make sense of the things that happen and how they fit together? Are we concerned about the price of all things but care nothing about the value of anything?

D. Do we seek out technology as the solution for every problem, as if we can fix and manipulate things better than we can understand and appreciate them?

V. An important consideration in this course involves the history of philosophy.

A. Initially, and almost until the 20th century, philosophical investigation involved the development of a systematic picture of the cosmos.

B. In the past two centuries, philosophy has moved to a concern with history and how we fit into the course and direction of history.

C. For many decades now, the academic discipline of philosophy has become more focused on specific, technical areas of investigation such as conceptual issues.

D. But technical philosophy has distanced many people because they prefer that philosophy concentrate on questions regarding core human concerns such as "the meaning of life."

VI. But philosophy can also be construed as the quest for guidance in the *Art of Living*, the pursuit of the very meaning of life and the means for attaining this meaning.

A. Classically, Socrates described philosophy as *learning how to die*, which implies coming to know what human life really *is*—not just how to live through it, but how to live it well.

B. More recently, the American philosopher John Dewey (1859–1952) claimed that philosophy only deserved attention and respect to the extent that it turned from dealing with the problems of philosophers and returned its attention to the problems of human beings.

C. Philosophy in this sense involves bringing things into question that may not have been questioned before, while also recognizing that the way in which these questions are being resolved will most likely reverberate back upon and influence our way of living.

D. In philosophy construed as a guide to living, there is an important difference between providing information and engendering a kind of engagement that elicits participation in the probing of issues and reflection on alternative ways of resolving them.

    1. Information is important, but it can compel a misleading objectivity in which you are brought into a formation of sorts, a common understanding where complying with this formation's dictates is more or less expected and becomes more important than probing more deeply into the issues.

    2. Philosophical engagement is anything but arbitrary and subjective. As we will see, it requires a rigor of its own, something we will hope to some extent to pursue together.

VII. Why have I chosen European philosophers on which to focus primarily in this course? Because they speak in important ways to the time in which we now find ourselves.

A. They are concerned with exploring the limits of human reason.

B. These philosophers tend also to pay close attention to our lives *in* the world, enmeshed in culture and engaged in a quest for significant opportunities for self-understanding and personal development.

C. These philosophers are also focused on the likely course of history. Does it have a direction?

VIII. In our time, various overlapping guides to living can be seen as reconfiguring in distinctive ways.

A. Reference to the past is giving way to hopes regarding the future, engendering the growing ascendancy of politics and economics.

1. The promise of biotechnologically driven human enhancement brings traditional values into question.
2. Economic outlooks have replaced more traditional ways of understanding the world, religious or political, for example.

B. Concerns regarding ways in which we are better able to be *in* the world are coming to dominate concerns regarding ways that we are not altogether *of* the world.
1. The transporting features of "high" culture are receiving commercial retranslation through mass-marketability motivations.
2. Medical avenues receive an emphasis and extension previously granted primarily to religion.

IX. In the course of our pending journey, we will consider four basic themes from a historical and thematic standpoint.

A. It has been said that though we are *in* we are not altogether *of* the world. This notion, the *axial* understanding of human life, underwent significant challenge when thinkers in the 18th-century Enlightenment argued that all superstitions be conquered through reason and knowledge.

B. It has been said as well that fundamental themes of human concern increasingly revolve more around meaning and meaninglessness than around guilt and innocence or immortality versus extinction.

C. A controversy has emerged over the asking of questions regarding meaning. Even if carefully pursued, are these sorts of questions expansive of our humanity or symptomatic of some kind of illness or malaise?

D. Finally, what is the nature and status of human reason since the Enlightenment? Has reason come to be understood as a means of resolving *all* issues? Or might there be alternative means?

Essential Reading:

Francis Fukuyama, *The End of History and the Last Man.*

Charles Taylor, *Sources of the Self: The Making of the Modern Identity.*

Supplementary Reading:

Hannah Arendt, *The Human Condition*.

Richard Tarnas, *The Passion of the Western Mind*.

Questions to Consider:

1. What roles can philosophy play in understanding life's meaning?

2. How does Enlightenment thinking challenge axial thinking?

Lecture One—Transcript
The Axial Model

Throughout the course of this lecture series, I'll be taking you on a journey. It's going to be an unusual journey in certain respects, and I want to outline its contours and some of the uncommon features before we begin. We're going to be looking at whether there may be a deeper meaning to life than we ordinarily experience and whether philosophy can help us to determine what that meaning might be. Now, some are going to say no, and they might say that such matters come down to whether we're healthy, whether we enjoy life, and whether we're successful. Others might feel that such matters really are private and belong to the realm of religion. During our journey together, we will respect those views, but we're going to follow a different path, a philosophical path.

There are three fundamental questions we must ask within the context of philosophy. Is reliable knowledge of our human nature possible? In fact, do human beings even have a nature? In a time such as ours, perhaps far less superstitious than disenchanted, what might be the human predicament? Is there one? Can human life be lived with both integrity and fulfillment, and might philosophy help us to find that integrity and fulfillment? Some of the issues we will discuss together are pretty complicated and controversial, but I hope to present a number of perspectives with which to engage. No one could agree with all of them, so if you agree with some of these views as we go along, I hope you'll genuinely value them and, hopefully, be enriched by them. If you disagree with some of the views that we'll be looking at, I do hope you'll still dwell with them, if only to stimulate your thinking even further.

Let's look for a moment at the backdrop from which the sorts of ideas that are going to be concerning us arose. We start with an ancient model. I'm going to be calling it the axial model. It was developed somewhere between 800 and 200, before the Common Era, in roughly a 600-year period. In the axial mode a sharp distinction was made between this world and some kind of a beyond, and the idea arose that although we are *in* this world, we are not altogether *of* this world. On this model, the axial model, human life is considered a journey that leads from appearance to reality, from bondage to liberation, from confusion to insight and from darkness to light. In the 18th century we come to the Enlightenment Period; Enlightenment was a challenge to this axial notion. When it was thought important to abandon the past and all old beliefs and superstitions, it moved to a determination that our own human reason is the instrument through which lives find their paths to meaning. In fact, we're going to be looking at some big pictures as we continue, rather than focusing narrowly on specifically defined technical problems. For example, we'll look at what human beings in past centuries were concerned about. For example, in the ancient world, the great human concern, perhaps, was death—how the fact that we die affects us and forces us to understand life. We will note a time—it's often associated with the Protestant Reformation—when the overarching human concern was guilt. Are we doing the right thing? What ought we do? Why do we not always do the right thing? In our time, and I think especially starting near the beginning of the 20th century, we arrive at a concern with meaning and that will be core to our reflections together. It becomes not a question of rightness or wrongness, but rather, what it is that really matters. What is it that truly has meaning? Is there anything worth doing? Is there anything that is genuinely meaningful?

Another big picture suggests that you start with the philosophy of Plato, one of the great philosophers of the Western world. He was, in fact, a great believer that we are not of this world, a philosopher who distinguished between appearance and reality. If we're to believe one line of thought, the relentless development of Western thought brings us, eventually, to a world where technology triumphs. This is a world where technology is viewed more and more as the solution to everything and where human life, therefore, is altogether *in* this world and does not have a home elsewhere. Still another view leads to Nietzsche who said that Western thoughts developed in such a way that sources of significant experience are dwindling, and therefore there are fewer and fewer things that matter. In short, this view says that meaning, in a deeper sense, no longer has any grounding.

Let me pause and reflect on this with you. There have been pictures—one of which is suggested that the deepest of human issues is that our life ends another—that we are, in some way—this has often been associated with religions—imbued with a guilt that we cannot understand and we can't understand how to overcome it either. A more contemporary concern has been a concern with what life means and whether it has a meaning, and it is this concern that we will be reflecting on. We'll be asking and wondering together whether philosophy can help us to pursue the path of determining whether life has meaning, and even whether the question "whether life has meaning" is a legitimate one.

Let's now continue. Ours is really an uncertain time—I think we all know that—when everything is getting questioned. We're concerned about politics, we have great, growing economic concerns, and we live in a world now where more and more it seems there are continuous natural disasters. We can't help notice controversies about the nature and the future of religion and seeming wars between religions, and underlying this has to be among other things, for any of us, a desire to find an overview. We want a way of looking at things that makes sense, helps us to see how we got to where we are and whether there's a way out of the situation that some worry we might be in. When the axial model was in place, people understood themselves on a journey of life. That journey of life, as I indicated, was from appearance to reality. It was meant to be a liberating journey and it was to bring us to a kind of insight, an insight about what mattered and thereby, we'd be touched and touched by meaning. When the Enlightenment came—and here I'm thinking primarily about the Enlightenment of the 18th century, which is said to have begun in France—reason, human reason, came to replace faith and tradition. Now do we live in a world where we have no overview? Do we have no schema to make sense of the things that happen and how they fit together? Have we become concerned about the price of all things, but the value of nothing? Has something happened that's unfolded through the 18th century Enlightenment that has brought us to the position where we seek out technology as the solution for every problem? As if it can fix and manipulate things better than we could, when all is said and done, understand and appreciate them.

An important consideration in this course involves the history of philosophy. Initially, and almost until the 20th century, philosophical investigation involved the development of a systematic picture of the cosmos, where we fit into things and what the nature and connection of things was. In the past two centuries, philosophy has moved to a concern with history and how we fit into the course and direction of history. In fact, for the 19th century especially, there was a great concern to articulate and understand a pattern to history, that if we could understand that pattern, maybe then we could fit in or at least see what the direction of the human spirit was. For many decades now, the academic discipline of philosophy has become more focused on specific, technical areas of investigation, primarily on conceptual issues. In fact, some time ago, Bertrand Russell said that philosophy had become the systematic abuse of technical terms that had specifically been invented for that purpose. William James actually once said that, "Philosophy was the search in a dark room for a black cat that wasn't there," and I'll have to admit to you that once on an airplane flight when my seat mate found out that I was a philosophy professor, that person said, "Well, then, tell me what some of your sayings are." Conceptual technical philosophy does not get so much involved; it is a very, very, technical pursuit, an articulate one. At the same time, it's one that requires a great deal of intricate analysis, but it is true that technical philosophy has distanced itself from many people because they prefer philosophy that concentrates on questions regarding core human concerns such as the meaning of life, and they think that philosophy owes us a reflection on those concerns.

Philosophy can actually do that and that's what we're going to be exploring in our time together. You see, philosophy can also be construed in our time not just as a technical discipline; it can also be construed as guidance in the art of living, the pursuit of the very meaning of life, and the means for attaining this meaning. There have been examples of this from the past; it isn't as if philosophy has just recently taken on these questions. Philosophy, throughout its history, has been far less technical, far more absorbed in questions about what it is it to be a human, and what am I to do to fully experience and to achieve the meaning of human life. Think back for a moment on Socrates, considered by many to be the father of Western philosophy. He described philosophy as a learning of how to die. What he meant by that, what he implied, was coming to know what human life really is—not just how to live through it, but how to live it well. More recently—and this one is close to my heart and you'll best keep this in mind as we continue—the American philosopher John Dewey, who lived from about 1859–1952, claimed that philosophy only deserved attention and respect if it no longer considered just technical problems, if it turned from dealings with, what Dewey called, the problems of philosophers, and returned its attention to the pressing problems of human beings.

Philosophy, in this sense, involves bringing things into question that maybe hadn't been questioned before, and it also involves recognizing that the way in which these questions eventually get resolved isn't going to be some abstract piece of knowledge we get. How these deep philosophical questions of what the meaning of life might get resolved will reverberate upon, make a difference in and influence the way in which we ourselves live our lives. We can't distance ourselves from questions about the meaning of life if we reflect on them philosophically. They're never meant to be just abstract concerns. They're meant to be taken as a way that we have to think about them and if we think about them seriously, our life is most likely, in some ways, to be changed. In philosophy that's construed as a guide to living there is an important difference. We can hardly dwell on this enough. There's an important difference between providing information and, on the other hand, engendering a kind of engagement with fundamental questions and issues. If we do that at all successfully, what it's going to make us do is participate in the probing of some of these issues and a reflecting on alternative ways of solving them. Obviously, information is important. It is terribly important that we have information, but it can compel a kind of misleading objectivity, an objectivity where you just stand back and look at things. You put things into some kind of objective formation and you develop, in a careful way, a common understanding, but as you do this, what happens is that you find yourself complying with a kind of system. You find yourself complying with the formation and what it dictates, and in the midst of gathering that information and putting it together systematically, what often fails to happen is a deep and more probing investigation of the underlying issues.

We need to keep in mind that philosophical engagement—and that's exactly what I hope that we can have together—is not arbitrary. It's not just a sharing of opinions; it's not merely subjective. As we're going to see, it requires a rigor and a care of its own, and it's something that I hope we can pursue together and by that, I mean that I hope that the questions that I bring up with you are questions that you will think about and you will wonder about. As you think about them, perhaps sometimes thinking they're very complex, and other times too simple, I hope that the very thinking about them will draw you to say, "Well, should this make a difference to how I think? Should this make a difference to how I see the world?" I've chosen some particular philosophers to be the means through which we will undertake our journey and, particularly, I've chosen some European philosophers on which to focus primarily in the course of what I hope will be our journey together. You might well ask, "Why has he chosen these particular philosophies and how is it that they turn out to be primarily European philosophers?" It's because I think they speak in important ways to the time in which we now find ourselves. One of these philosophers, Hegel, who we'll be talking about soon and who lived from 1770–1831, said, "Philosophy is the child of its time." He also said, "Philosophy is its time comprehended in thought." What I believe is that these European philosophers and their philosophies reflected their time and that they did so in different ways. Plus, they didn't agree with each other, catch up and comprehend their time in thought. What I believe is the case is that today—the now in which we live, the now we hope to understand—is, in many ways, the consequence of what these European philosophers and their strange, revealing, unusual ways, said about what life in the world was like.

For example, they, as a group disagreeing with each other, were concerned to explore the limits of human reason. Remember I told you that the Enlightenment Period of the 18th century wanted to get beyond what they thought of as tradition and superstition, wanted simply to focus and rely on reason. These European philosophers we'll be talking about together take that as a starting point. As we're going to see, though, they worry very much about what reason is capable of, what it can do if we must rely on it, what hope can we truly have? One might think, perhaps, that we can't rely on human reason. We must jump back to faith. We must go some other route. These European philosophers, who we have to think of in ways as contemporary because they take reason so seriously, do insist that wherever we go, we start with reason. That is important for us to keep in mind in any pathway we take toward understanding the meaning of our time, and whether our time offers meaning in life.

Now, these same European philosophers also tended to pay close attention to their lives in the world, enmeshed in culture, questing after significant opportunities for self-understanding and personal development. They did not just analyze concepts. I don't mean to depreciate the careful, technical, conceptual analysis of ideas. That's important. It's a part of professional philosophy. But, these philosophers we'll be talking about together, though they also did that sort of technical thing, they also focused on concrete human life in the world. Additionally, they also focused on the likely course of history. Marx, for instance—whom we'll be talking about—as is commonly known, thought that revolution was the future. Michele Foucault, a French philosopher of the 20th century, thought that there were dramatic changes that happened periodically in history. Peter Drucker, who is in the School of Management and is considered by many a great thinker living in our time, said that "Particular times would come," and Drucker thinks we're in one now, "where a dramatic change will occur where people living 20 years from now," the early 21st century, "will look back on us and hardly recognize us in the same way that looking forward we could not even imagine what they may be like."

In our time, there have been various overlapping guides to living and they can be seen as reconfiguring the way we understand life in very distinctive ways. For example, reference to the past, which has been so much a part of us we call it our heritage, is giving way to hopes regarding the future. There's been a growing ascendancy of political values and economic theories as providing the rubric, the framework, for understanding life now, its opportunity and its hopes. Another thing that has happened is that we have seen, and we're going to see more of, biotechnologically driven, human-enhancement opportunities, where, through biotechnology, human life might be altered, enhanced, or changed in significant ways, and that will dramatically bring into question traditional values. It may well be the case, also that general economic outlooks, economic theories, theories of the world of money, have replaced, in important ways, more traditional ways of understanding life in the world—religious or political ones, for example. It's actually quite possible that we are living under a tyranny of the economic metaphor and we'll have some reflection on that. There are other concerns that emerge, too, and they regard ways in which we are better able to be in the world and less to think of any other notion of world, literal or metaphorical. These ways of being in the world are coming to dominate concerns, rather than allow us to reflect more in perhaps transcendent dimensions to ourselves that might be hidden from ourselves.

We see a variety of things that are puzzling. I think we know them well, in one sense, but I think we should dwell on them and they should concern us. We know that the transporting features of high culture that many celebrate have progressively received commercial retranslation through mass marketing. We know that the notion of the lower and the higher, as it applies to culture, has altered in such a way that everything has been meant to be made easily available, and maybe in being made easily available—some people actually use this phrase—we've been "dumbed down," something has been lost. We also know—we can hardly avoid knowing it by looking at popular magazines, in many ways, informative magazines—that medical avenues and ideas have received more and more emphasis. They've received an emphasis and an extension that was previously granted primarily to religion. More and more, we hear about medicine as the cure for all kinds of things that in the past we might have thought of as just simply part of life.

In the course of our journey, which we are about to undertake, we'll be considering four basic things and we're going to look at them from an historical standpoint—how we came to have these themes upon us as ones that we need to reflect on. Also, we're going to be looking at some of the themes that are open to us thematically, not just historically. It's been said that, though we are *in* it, we're not altogether *of* the world. This notion, this axial understanding of human life as I mentioned at the beginning of our time together, was significantly impacted by 18th-century philosophical thinking. It was impacted by what we've called the 18th century Enlightenment and its emphasis that we must conquer superstition through reason and knowledge. We need to look at this and understand its implications. As well, it's often been said that fundamental themes of human concern increasingly revolve more and more around meaningful and meaninglessness, rather than around guilt and innocence, or questions about immortality versus extinction. A controversy has also emerged over the very asking of questions about meaning. Is the asking of questions about meaning a necessary avenue to take to a better understanding of the depth of life and the possibilities of life? Or is it possible that asking questions about what life means actually indicates that, perhaps, we suffer from some unfortunate illness? We, perhaps, have not matured.

We are in various kinds of situations that oppress us and to compensate for that, we ask questions about the meaning of life. Some will say questions about the meaning of life are necessary to ask for us to be truly human. Others will say that the asking of them indicates that something has gone wrong, and we only ask them because we are in, perhaps, a not-comprehended form of trouble. We'll need to look into that. Are these valid questions? Or, is it symptomatic of some other kind of trouble that we would ask the questions at all?

Finally, what is the nature and status of human reason since the Enlightenment? Has reason come to be understood as a means of resolving all questions or might there be alternative means? From out of the concentration and celebration of reason in the 18th century, a number of philosophers have actually looked at, through and beyond human reason. They've come up with different and, in some ways, extraordinary ways to think about and to walk the path toward answers to what life means. We'll be looking at these matters and all these questions in a careful way, as we move forward in our time together.

Lecture Two
Kant's Hopeful Program

Scope:

Philosophy has been understood in two overlapping ways: as a means to knowledge and as a guide to living. The latter arises out of a particular understanding of human life, *viz.*, the *axial* model. In its terms, human life is a journey through darkness to light and from appearance to reality. To the degree that the journey is successful, human life is delivered from bondage to liberation. Representative samples of the axial model at work in Western philosophy are reviewed before a turn is made to the beginning of the collapse of this model during the Enlightenment (c. 1750) and most notably in the writings of Immanuel Kant (1724–1804). The crisis that Kant inaugurates is explored through his account of what metaphysics is, why we must pursue it, what our reason demands yet also prevents us from achieving, and what obstacles deter us from comprehending human life as an axial journey. Finally, Kant states succinctly three intertwined questions that shadow any philosophical attempt to provide a guide to living: *What can we know? What ought we do? For what can we hope?*

Outline

I. In the axial mode, human life is understood as involving a journey in which those who are successful move from a Lower to a Higher Realm. This journey is central to the meaning of life.

A. Through an elevated mode of knowing, the world as we ordinarily experience it is left largely behind, deemed lesser if not illusory, and the domain of reality itself is approached.

1. Often a quite disciplined nonmystical analytical training is construed as a prerequisite for the ultimate kind of knowledge sought, the Higher Realm.

2. Ultimate knowledge typically is understood as both transformative and incommunicable.

B. The Lower Realm is construed as an arena of bondage, either the consequence of ignorance of higher realities, or the result of enslavement to various passions that confuse and distract us.

  1. In sustained contact with reality, we are understood to have become liberated, one with our true selves, and thus to have become who we really are.

  2. To have become one's true Self is to have become Good, and to be in this sense Good is said to bring happiness.

C. A significant and pivotal distinction is made between living in confusion—however unwittingly—and the attaining of insight, often called *Enlightenment*.

  1. Initial insight can often be fleeting and itself somewhat baffling. It may only reorient the traveler on the axial journey. The life of Socrates provides a paradigmatic example of initial insight. His moment of initial insight came when he was told that he was the wisest of the Athenians. He doubted this assertion, so he began asking questions that set him on a new path of personal discovery.

  2. Final and sustainable Enlightenment is typically construed as involving an arduous discipline and has as a consequence the viewing of the ordinary and everyday world differently.

D. The axial understanding of human life is found in a pervasive ocular imagery that is endemic both to religion and to philosophy: the quest to move out of darkness (the Bad) and into the light (the Good).

  1. Sight has been given a priority in philosophy that has tended to make philosophical guides to living primarily matters of the intellect.

  2. Axially (and somewhat inexplicably) the realm of light was deemed unchanging, thus reliable and *the* foundation for all human wisdom and successful activity.

  3. Light, liberation, and reality came to fuse as the sought after, hidden foundation of *everything*. Reaching it meant salvation itself.

II. Paradoxically, the Enlightenment of the 18th century, a watershed event in the West, was in crucial respects contrary to the traditional "Enlightenment" as embedded and understood within the axial mode.

   A. The "highest" kind of knowing the axial vision offered—intuition—came to be viewed negatively and dismissively.

   1. What passed as wisdom was construed most typically as the remains of superstition.

   2. Frequently, a "higher" knowing was debunked as mystification and/or a disguised means of reaffirming and protecting the privileges of various elites.

   3. Higher knowledge was often construed as the stale residue of traditions and customs no longer relevant to the modern world.

   B. The emerging empirical sciences were taken as the paradigms of knowing.

   1. Humans themselves came increasingly to be viewed as proper "objects" of scientific knowledge.

   2. Humans were seen as altogether *in this* world and not of any other realm except in the most extended and metaphorical of senses.

   C. Knowledge came more and more to be coupled with power and was construed as an instrument for controlling the world, not as a means of transcending its ordinariness in a journey toward a Higher Realm.

   1. Liberation became more a concern with freedom *from* interference than the attainment of oneness with one's axial true Self.

   2. The qualitative notion of fulfillment eroded in the face of the quantitative pursuit of pleasure.

III. The watershed work of Immanuel Kant (1724-1804) can be understood as an attempt to reconcile the dynamics and hopes of the axial mentality with the data and opportunities made available through developing modern science.

   A. Kant distinguishes two quite distinct and equally important understandings of metaphysics, both of which he claims to be vital to our comprehension of our human futures.

1. Metaphysics can be construed as itself a science, a systematic organization of our knowledge of that which we encounter as existing *beyond* the world of our direct worldly experience.

2. Metaphysics in this sense, as a science, Kant claims to be beyond our human capacity. Regarding the existence of axial reality, Kant is thus officially agnostic.

3. Kant also understands metaphysics as a natural disposition of the human "soul," exhibiting itself in the unavoidable urge to ask questions regarding our human nature and destiny, the existence of a power or powers beyond us, and the overall intelligibility of the universe as a whole.

4. *Kant claims that we are only fully human to the degree that we ask these questions.* Their philosophical pursuit itself offers guidance in living, even if they will not yield to scientific investigation.

B. Following tradition, Kant claims that there are but two avenues for knowing. One is human reason. The other is by means of our sensibility, primarily through our senses.

1. Kant understands reason as interpretive, not as capable of directly revealing reality without distortion.

2. Kant also claims that reason generates certain ideas that he believes to be inescapable, yet rationally irresolvable.

IV. The cognitive legacy of Kant is to give comfort to the axial mind, yet to deny claims that humans can have rational insight into metaphysical realities.

A. Philosophy now bifurcates into the analytical investigation of concepts on the one hand and alternative reflections on the meaning of life on the other.

B. A central question arises regarding how (and what kind of) human freedom might fit into this axial, scientific, and philosophical understanding of our life *in* the world.

C. A further question arises regarding how philosophy might actually provide guidance to life under the circumstances Kant outlines.

V. As previously mentioned, Kant believes that there are two avenues to know reality: reason, which we have already discussed, and the senses.

A. Kant says our senses are tied to physical things and can reveal the physical, but that we have no extrasensory capacity.

B. Our Western tradition says that we see this world solely through our senses and that we have no sense that allows us to see beyond this world.

C. Kant offers the notion of unanswerable questions that our senses and our scientific knowledge cannot comprehend: Do we have a soul? Is there a power beyond us—God perhaps? Can this power tell us what will happen to us after this life ends?

D. Kant finally poses the three most fundamental questions that we all must ask:

   1. What can I know?

   2. Given the limits of my reason, what ought I do?

   3. For what can I hope?

Essential Reading:

Sebastian Gardner, *Routledge Philosophy Guidebook to Kant and the Critique of Pure Reason*.

Peter Gay, *The Enlightenment: An Interpretation*, Volume II: *The Science of Freedom*.

Supplementary Reading:

Immanuel Kant, *Critique of Pure Reason*.

P. F. Strawson, *The Bounds of Sense, An Essay of Kant's Critique of Pure Reason*.

Questions to Consider:

1. What are some of the different ways in which the axial model understands the journey of life?

2. How does Kant understand metaphysics and assess the possibility of its pursuit?

Lecture Two—Transcript
Kant's Hopeful Program

During our first time together, and I'm happy you're here with me, we asked whether there could be a question about the meaning of life that would be an important one to ask, and we also begun our consideration of whether philosophy might have something to say about that question of the meaning of life. Additionally, we made a distinction between philosophy as a technical discipline and philosophy as, perhaps, a way of offering guidance in living. Let's consider and continue our reflections together.

In the axial mode, which we met before, human life is understood as involving a journey in which those who are successful move from a lower realm to a higher realm, and it's this journey that is understood as central to the meaning of life. Whatever the meaning of life is, this journey, this axial journey from appearance to reality, from this realm to another, from bondage to liberation, is very, very important. What was thought through the axial mind was that some elevated way of knowing the world as we ordinarily experience, it could maybe be left temporarily behind, and that the world as we ordinarily know it could be viewed as lesser, and that it could be viewed, if not as illusory, yet not quite as the domain of reality itself, when reality came to be approached. In fact, the philosophy of Plato and Platonism generally exemplifies this way of thinking. Often, a quite disciplined, non-mystical, analytical, even conceptual training was construed by this axial mind, at least among its philosophers, as a prerequisite, as an important thing to do in order for the ultimate kind of knowledge sought to be found. Ultimate knowledge was typically understood as both transformative and, in many instances, it was also understood to be incommunicable. The lower realm was construed as an arena of bondage, and the bondage could be construed as either a consequence of ignorance of what the higher realities actually were or sometimes as the result of enslavement to various passions that would confuse and distract us. Supposedly, in a sustained contact with reality, we're understood to have become liberated, one with our true selves and, thus, to have become who we really are. Only if we became who we really are, it was thought, could we have attained or be in the vicinity of the meaning of life. To have become our true selves was viewed on this axial model as to have become good. To be good, in this sense, was said to bring happiness. Now, this happiness would indicate that life's meaning had been found or we were close to finding it, though the happiness would not itself be construed as the meaning of life—a symptom of nearing it, but not the meaning of life itself.

A significant and pivotal distinction comes to be made between living in confusion, however unwittingly, and the attaining of a special insight that was, in fact, often called *enlightenment*. Not Enlightenment in the 18th century sense that we referred to before, but a special insight or enlightenment at the end of the axial journey. Now, this insight could often take the form of something that was fleeting and was even experienced, in some ways, as baffling. For some, what the initial enlightenment or insight would do would be just to reorient the traveler on the axial journey, and the life of Socrates actually provides a kind of paradigmatic example of this kind of initial insight. It's a curious story. He was, in fact, told that he was the wisest of all the Athenians. He didn't see this to be the case at all, but having been told that reoriented him. He came to question whether he really was wise and, in Athens, began asking questions that set him on his path to the discovery that in fact, well, controversially so, maybe he truly was the wisest person in Athens and in touch with a higher realm. It's also true that the Hindu gurus who became dispellers of darkness often said that early in their lives, they had a kind of strange experience that reoriented them and turned them on a path to a final enlightenment.

Final and sustainable insight, revelation enlightenment, is typically construed as involving an arduous discipline and, as a consequence, viewing the ordinary and everyday world quite differently. The enlightenment that comes is not necessarily just seeing something else. It's also seeing the ordinary world being enlightened in an extraordinary way. The axial understanding of life is always involved in a kind of pervasive ocular imagery and that's been part of our religious heritage and part of philosophy, as well. The quest is always construed as moving out of darkness, the bad, into light, which is construed as the good. Sight, visual sighting, has been given a priority in philosophy that has tended to make philosophical modes of enlightenment and philosophical guidance, primarily, matters of the intellect. In terms of the axial model, and it's hard to finally make sense of this, the realm of light is viewed as unchanging. It's viewed as reliable and, finally, as the foundation for all human wisdom and successful activity. Light, liberation and reality come to fuse, they come to be one in the same, and they come to be seen as the hidden foundation of everything. To reach that was viewed as salvation, as having found the meaning of life itself.

Now, paradoxically, and it is a paradox, the Enlightenment of the 18th century—not enlightenment as something that comes at the end of the axial journey, but the Enlightenment of the 18th century—was a watershed event in the Western world and so contrary to the traditional older view of enlightenment, that of enlightenment as a transforming insight that was embodied and understood within the axial picture. This new enlightenment is a notion of getting enlightened through reason—not a revelatory intuition that one got through reason and got into another realm, but a notion of reason that was very much focused into this world. In terms of that 18th century notion of reason, what had been offered as wisdom was now construed most typically as the remains of superstition, as something that belonged to the Church, viewed negatively, or to the priestly class. Frequently, some higher-enlightened notion of knowing was debunked, was viewed as simple mystification or a kind of a disguised means of reaffirming and protecting the privileges of various elite groups. Higher knowledge was often construed as the stale residue of traditions and customs no longer relevant to the then modern world of the 18th century. In fact, the empirical sciences came to be taken as the paradigms of knowing, sciences that would know this world and gradually—and this took a number of centuries to work itself out and it reaches our times—humans themselves came to be viewed increasingly as proper objects of scientific knowledge. Humans slowly, yet progressively, came to be viewed as altogether *in* this world and not *of* any other world, except in the very most extended and metaphorical sense. Knowledge came, more and more, to be coupled with power and to be construed as an instrument for controlling the world, not as a means of transcending this world and its ordinariness, not as a means of undertaking a journey to some higher realm.

Liberation became, more and more, a concern with freedom from interference, as one went about what one did in this world. It became, less and less, liberation in the sense of finding a way to be liberated to go on a journey that would take one to the discovery of one's true self. In fact, the qualitative notion of transforming fulfillment eroded. It eroded in the face of the notion of a quantitative pursuit of pleasures that, in fact, were to be found in this world. So, if you think about this for a moment before we move on, there is a notion of reason we inherit. It's an axial notion of reason as a means of taking a journey to a higher form of life and enlightenment, but a notion of reason replaces this in the 18th century. In the 18th century period that is also called an "Enlightenment," that new notion of reason is one that is directed toward this world finding means of how to control this world and, in the course of that, liberating oneself to be more and more able to pursue the things of this world.

We now come to the philosopher Kant, who is very clearly the watershed thinker who will influence a great deal of how we came to reflect on these matters. Kant lived from 1724–1804 and he may be seen as an attempt to reconcile the dynamics and hopes of this axial mentality that construed life as a journey, a journey toward what might be thought of as the meaning of life. Kant tried to reconcile that with the opportunities that were being made available through developing modern science. Kant distinguishes between two distinct and equally important understandings of a discipline called metaphysics, both of which he claimed to be vital to our comprehension of our human futures. We should dwell on this for a moment because the notion of metaphysics is a very, very important notion for us to grasp. Metaphysics was construed by the philosophical tradition as the pursuit of that which is beyond this world. The Greek word *meta* has as one of its meanings, beyond. Of course the question would be can there be a pursuit that is metaphysical? Can there be a pursuit that would take us beyond the physical world? Kant, in his own reflections, distinguished two notions of metaphysics. One was metaphysics as a science, which meant a systematic organization of a kind of knowledge you could get through directly encountering things. But, Kant thought that the notion of metaphysics, that we could have scientific metaphysics based on an encounter with things beyond the physical world, was impossible. He thought it was impossible because he thought reason could not reach beyond the physical world. It could reach no metaphysical world. So, in that sense, Kant told us that metaphysics, as a science, as a study of a scientific type that would give us encounter and knowledge of things beyond the physical world, was impossible because he said reason simply couldn't reach beyond the physical world.

Still, Kant did not necessarily deny that there was something beyond the physical world. He didn't deny that there could be a truth to the axial mentality. To say that metaphysics couldn't be a science is not to say that there may not be something beyond the physical world. Kant, in fact, regarding that issue, was in a curious, almost coy way at times, agnostic. What he said was that he was limiting reason to make room for faith. What that meant for him—let's pause on it for a moment—what that meant for him was that he was showing that reason could not stretch beyond the physical world, but if it couldn't stretch beyond the physical world, it couldn't know whether there was anything beyond the physical world. It could neither prove that there was nor prove that there wasn't. If you showed reason couldn't prove there was or there wasn't, you had limited reason's reach. Then Kant could say, "Ah, in having done that, I've left room for faith."

Kant did have another understanding of metaphysics, an important understanding that will be at the core of our reflections as we consider whether it makes sense to talk about life having a meaning and whether it makes sense talking about philosophy as a guide. It's important as a way of pursuing whether life has a meaning and what that meaning might be because Kant also understood metaphysics as a natural disposition of the human soul. It exhibits itself in the unavoidable urge he claimed that we have to ask questions regarding our human nature, regarding our destiny as human beings, regarding whether there may be a power or powers beyond the physical world, and whether they may be a kind of grand intelligibility to the universe as a whole. What Kant said was that to be fully human, you have to be asking these questions. If you think about it for a moment, this is strange. We can only use reason and reason cannot reach beyond the physical world, but we are only fully human, we're only really human beings, if nonetheless, in the face of the inability of the one instrument we have, reason, we nonetheless continue to ask these questions. We continue to ask, "What is the meaning life? Is there a power beyond us? What is the ultimate destiny of our soul—if we have one—or of our life after our death, and does the totality of the cosmos fit into some intelligible order?"

Kant was telling us we have to be rational and if we're fully rational, we do find that reason is limited. Not only do we have to be fully rational, we have to realize reason is our one hope. He then told us that it could extend just so far, that the questions that matter were beyond its reach, but we have to ask these questions anyway. Now, following tradition, Kant claimed that there are but two avenues through which we could know. One, we've already looked at; that's reason. The other avenue is our senses, our sensibility. Now, Kant understood reason, as among other things, to be a means of interpreting, never reaching beyond the world, but interpreting what we experience in the world, but certainly not capable of revealing reality without distortion. As we've seen, Kant also claimed that reason generated ideas that he believed to be inescapable and not rationally resolvable. The cognitive legacy of Kant is to give comfort to the axial mind, yet to deny that humans can have rational insight into any metaphysical realities. As a result, philosophy now bifurcates; it splits into an analytical investigation of concepts. Kant thought that philosophy could serve science and philosophy could also analyze concepts that are used in all areas of our life. Philosophy then separately—and in this strange way that can't be satisfying if satisfaction means finding provable answers—philosophy can also reflect, as supposedly we must if we're to be fully human, on questions regarding meaning. A central question arises in the midst of this. How and what kind of human freedom might fit into a scientific understanding of how our life is lived only in the world? Kant gave a great deal of reflection, which we are going to be concerning ourselves with, on how our life in the world, about which he thought we may know a great deal, accommodates the need we have and the assumption that we are truly free beings. Kant came to be concerned with how to understand freedom and if our rational mind could only deal directly with the world that we find ourselves in, in this world, how can we sort out what freedom is like and what its rational features are.

Further questions arise regarding how philosophy might actually provide guidance for living under the circumstances that Kant outlined. Let me give you a few examples of this that I think will further clarify what we're going to be looking at together. I hope you'll notice that I said that Kant believed there were two avenues, and only two avenues, by means of which we could hope to know reality. One we've looked at and that is reason. The other, Kant said, are our senses. What did Kant says about our senses? What Kant told us was that our senses are tied to physical things and can only reveal physical things. That means that we don't have an extrasensory sense that might allow us to leap out and beyond the world we find ourselves in, leap out beyond it, and find a metaphysical reality. You see, the entire Western tradition that we are so caught up in believes that it's our senses that allow us to see the world, but we have no sense that allows seeing anything that would be viewed as beyond the world. Someone might rightly ask, and some of the philosophers we are going to be looking at after Kant, are going to suggest that, quite possibly, we do have some extra sense, a sense that is not simply tied to this world, but allows us, in some way, to go beyond this world. Unfortunately, the tradition in Kant simply is the culmination of this tradition that tells that we have no such sense. It's just simply not available to us and, therefore, what he offered us was the notion of these unanswerable questions that even our senses— and that implies what scientific investigation could provide in the way of knowledge for us—even our senses and our scientific knowledge couldn't reach.

He said that we have to ask if we have a soul. Does this have a soul after we die? That's a special metaphysical question that we simply can't avoid. He said that we have to ask, we can't get around asking, we experience it even if we try to mute it, is there a power somehow beyond us? A power—now, the traditional word for that would be God—is there a power beyond us to which we might enter into a relationship? What might that relationship be? What would that tell us about what our life might be like after this life we are living ends? Kant also said, however speculative it is, we cannot help but to ask questions about how the universe began. We can't help but to ask questions about where the universe might be going. We must be modern people. We must live in a world where we realize that science gives what knowledge we can receive but, nonetheless, we can't just move away from these other questions. Do I have something about me that lives beyond this physical life? Is there a power beyond me? Not an indifferent power, but a power in relation to how whatever happens to me after this life will be determined? Am I just a chance occurrence in the universe or is there an origin to the universe, a destiny and direction to it, and I've got to understand what this origin and what this destiny are if I'm even to understand my place, my circumstance, my meaning in life?

Having limited reason, what Kant finally said was that there are three fundamental questions that we absolutely have to ask. What can I truly and finally know? Given the limits of my reason, what as a human being ought I then do based on how little or how much I am able to know—what ought I do as a human being living in this world? And Kant offered us the final question—for what, when all is said and done, can I hope? What genuine, realistic hope can I have for my life? He concluded that if you take those three questions— what can I know, what ought I do, and for what might I hope—and fuse them together, they're really one question—what does it mean to be human. You can only begin to be human if you ask what it means to be human. We'll look into Kant a bit further as we continue on our journey together.

Lecture Three
The Kantian Legacy

Scope:

Kant claims to have demonstrated the limits to our knowledge, even of ourselves, yet makes many arresting claims regarding our human nature. By what right and by what means does he do this? Particularly crucial is his assertion that at our core is something he calls imagination, a "blind but indispensable function of the soul." Equally important is his conception of the "I," our supposedly subjective self. Most central, however, is Kant's robust account of how our moral life ought to be led in the face of our irremediable ignorance of ultimate things. The consequences that this entails for our understanding of religion are explored.

Outline

I. A brief review of Kant's account of reason in relation to the enterprise of metaphysics will help us to understand Kant's complicated vision and his influential legacy.

    A. As a cognitive capacity, reason has at least two limiting aspects:

        1. The transcendental function of reason is to interpret human experience.

        2. Reason is also a generator of ideas that are inescapable and with which we must grapple, for example, the idea that there is an ultimate foundation to our experience.

    B. As we have seen in Lecture Two, Kant believes that the three main questions are: What can we know? What ought we do? For what can we hope? But he believes our reason is limited as a means of knowledge regarding the true nature of things.

        1. Reason gives rise to antinomies, especially regarding human freedom, when it makes claims about the whole of reality.

        2. Irresolvable, intellectual conflicts emerge when reason attempts to obtain knowledge of the true nature of the self—conflicts that Kant refers to as *paralogisms*.

II. Kant's particular account of reason as the core of a person's dimension was groundbreaking, but it raised problems for Kant's successors in a number of ways:

A. The standpoint from which Kant's examination of reason takes place is itself controversial.

    1. There is a conflict between the pervasively interpretive function of reason and its allegedly direct noninterpretive knowledge of itself.

    2. The notion that reason has a structure that is neither culturally nor historically bound is typical of Kant and the Enlightenment but is attacked as too abstract by many successors to the Enlightenment.

    3. The categories that Kant uses to explain things do not depend on the language used. Later philosophers claim that those who speak a different language may not have the same understanding.

B. Kant's account of the conceptual status of the "I," a notion he refers to as "the transcendental unity of apperception," is not an easy concept to understand. We will approach it as follows.

    1. Kant makes an important distinction between the concept of "I" and any supposedly Real Self that we are said to possess.

    2. Kant also distinguishes between the "I" and those empirical dimensions of the Self that are available to scientific investigation.

    3. Kant also distinguishes our true Selves, even though we cannot know our true Selves.

III. The notion of imagination is central to Kant's philosophy. It is somewhat obscure in Kant and has important implications for later philosophical reflections on possible meanings for human life.

A. Kant considered the imagination to be in a necessary relation to all of our acts of knowing. His account has complex implications for any understanding that we might generate regarding our human nature.

1. There is a central and perennial philosophical argument regarding the relation of formal structure to power or energy.
2. For Kant, imagination is problematically resistant to any rational comprehension.

B. Kant's use of the word "imagination" is both unfortunate and at the same time suggestive in promising ways.

1. The unavoidable conclusion is that what Kant labels as imagination must be a precognitive, mysterious, and even an irrational faculty.
2. Among the Romantics, imagination is intimately connected with creativity. In this respect, they, particularly Coleridge, claim inspiration from Kant.

IV. Kant's understanding of the moral life is central to his conception of our human nature and, of course, human freedom.

A. Human freedom is a necessary but theoretically unprovable assumption for the existence of any moral life at all.

B. Kant makes space available in his theoretical philosophy for the (problematic) presence of freedom.

C. Kant divides the human moral predicament into a battle between duty and inclination, between rationality and passion.

1. Kant's deontological stress is shown in his emphasis on rational motivation.
2. Kant distinguishes between hypothetical and categorical imperatives to action.
3. Kant offers alternative criteria for evaluating those maxims by which actions are decided upon in the moral sphere.

V. Religion has an important place in Kant's understanding of our human situation.

A. Kant's consideration of the notion of God, understood by him as an "absolutely necessary being," is controversial.

1. Kant rejects traditional proofs for God's existence.

2. Teleological concerns are hauntingly present in Kant's thought, for example, in his intrigue with the notion of internal purposiveness in the natural world.

3. Kant rejects ordinary and institutionally driven conceptions of God.

B. Kant places the fundamental elements of religion within a thoroughly rational conception of the demands of moral life.

1. The notion of immortality is a rational postulate.

2. Kant asserts that there must be an infinite period of time in which to make it possible for us to become perfect and morally pure.

3. The notion of God as a rational postulate has implausibilities for many.

VI. Kant's is an austere view, mixing reason with moral duty and viewing religion as arising from a rational conception of moral duty. It puzzles some and outrages others.

Essential Reading:

Frederick Beiser, *The Fate of Reason, German Philosophy from Kant to Fichte*.

Immanuel Kant, *Religion within the Limits of Reason Alone*.

Supplementary Reading:

Isaiah Berlin, *The Crooked Timber of Humanity*.

Immanuel Kant, *Groundwork on the Metaphysics of Morals*.

Questions to Consider:

1. What are the basic functions that Kant believes reason to have?

2. What is the role of imagination, according to Kant?

3. How does Kant understand the dynamics of our moral life?

Lecture Three—Transcript
The Kantian Legacy

We've been exploring together the notion of life as being a journey and with it the idea that there may be a goal to this journey—the discovery of the meaning of life—if, of course, there is a meaning. During the Enlightenment period of the 18th century, it came to be understood that if there was any guide at all for this journey, it would have to be reason and reason alone—not faith, not tradition and certainly not superstition.

The philosopher Kant, whom we've already looked at a bit, completely agreed that reason would need to be the guide. However, Kant understood reason, in fact, to be severely limited. But oddly, at the same time, he said there are questions we have to ask, questions about the meaning of life, and that we are only human if we ask those questions. Well, reason is limited, we must use reason and yet, meaning-of-life questions have to be asked and reason perhaps can't fully help us answer them. What do we do? Where do we stand? I think a brief review of Kant's account of reason in relation to the enterprise of metaphysics—the looking for something beyond the world as we know it—is bound to help us to understand Kant's somewhat complicated vision and his very influential legacy, as we are going to see.

Kant saw reason as a cognitive capacity, something we use to know things and as having two very important limitations. One of those limitations was that reason could only be used to interpret our experience. It could never know the way things truly are in themselves. Philosophers tend to use big words. Kant's word is "transcendental," that there is a transcendental function of reason that it interprets, but it never gives us full access to something called "reality." Kant also said that our reason generates ideas. That is to say, ideas emerge, which our minds are not equipped to deal with and to find answers to, but we are trapped by these ideas. We can't escape them. We have to ask them.

With Kant saying that we have to ask these questions and that these questions and ideas are unavoidable for us, we seem to be in a very, very difficult situation. Kant thinks that the three main questions are: What can I know? What ought I to do? For what can I hope? But when Kant claims that we are in the pursuit of those questions, he claims that we get into deep, deep difficulty. That is, that our reason gives rise to something he calls "antinomies." We might call these "contradictions."

For instance, if we ask the question: "Are we really free?" Do we have freedom? Kant says that if we assume we are free, contradictory consequences follow intellectually from believing we are free. But Kant says that if we assume we are not free, equally contradictory conclusions follow. So Kant thinks that shows that our reason is actually not equipped to deal with these matters. Further, he says that we can't help after all, but assume that the universe began at some time and that it is limited in circumference of space, but he says if we assume that, contradictions follow from that, and he says if we assume that time never had a beginning, and that space is boundless, then equally, contradictions arise.

Where does this leave us? If we assume we are free, contradictions follow. If we assume we are not free but our activities are determined, contradictions follow, and if we assume time had a beginning, contradictions follow. If we assume time never began, contradictions follow. Where does this leave us? Then Kant asks a question that is going to haunt us. It is going to bother us as we move along. He asks what we can say about our true nature. What are we really like? But remember, as I have already indicated, Kant says our reason can only interpret. But if it can't know what anything is like, then it also can't know what we ourselves are really like in ourselves.

I think, frankly, Kant never found a way to say something that was exciting and interesting in a literary way. He says this in that kind of conceptual way in which philosophers tend to say things. On the other hand, what Kant is doing in opening the door to claiming that we can't know what we are really like in our true nature; we only know ourselves as we interpret ourselves. Kant is opening up the possibility that there is a deep, deep mystery in what it means to be human. If we are going on a road together toward the meaning of life, if there is a meaningful life, and we can't even be sure what we are like as human beings, if Kant is right, then we only have our appearance to ourselves. We can't grasp our two-rule reality, how can we move toward the meaning of life then? How can we know there is one if we can't know what our true nature is, and every time we talk about things such as freedom or whether time had a beginning, we fall into contradictions?

Kant, in fact, says that if we try to prove things about our true nature, as opposed to how we appear to ourselves, we fall into something he calls *paralogisms*. What that simply means is that there are fallacies in reasoning, involved in every attempt to argue and prove what our real nature is. Bottom line on this: Kant says that everything we experience is through interpretation. We even interpret our experience of ourselves. Therefore, we never know our own true nature, only how we appear to ourselves, and if we are looking for the meaning of life, if we can't even know our own true nature, how should we be expected to determine what the meaning of life is? Clearly, we are in great difficulties from the standpoint of Kant's philosophy, and his particular account of reason, which says, "we must rely of it, it is our sole confident, our sole means of knowing," that account, when he tells us how limited our reason is, it creates a kind of collision.

What do we do in a situation where we must use our reason, we know it is limited, but we must ask these fundamental questions? This raises huge, huge problems for Kant's successors. Some people have even said that the history of Western philosophy after Kant—at least on the continent of Europe—involves philosophers saying Kant couldn't be right, but yet he says important things. Actually, that is the way you make a career, in a way of saying things that are very difficult, very controversial, perhaps even obscure. But if you can get people talking about you, you've got something going—and philosophers talk about Kant still today.

Let's consider some of the reflections, the reactions to Kant. For one thing, the question was asked, "What was the standpoint from which Kant spoke?" After all, what does Kant tell us? Kant says we interpret everything. We even interpret our encounters with ourselves. But if we even interpret our encounter with ourselves, then we only have an interpretation. Where does Kant stand when he even says such a thing? Is he above the fray? Does he have a special insight? How does he get to where he gets? What is his standpoint? Further, Kant talks as if our reason is the same in all historical periods, the same in all cultures. Is it possible that our reason is culture bound, that it is history bound, that our reason may be different in one part of the world than in another? Is it possible that when you really come down to it, that reason changes over history?

Critics of Kant, looking back, say, "Okay, we use our reason. It makes interpretations." But does it do it the same way, all the time, in all cultural settings? Perhaps not; perhaps Kant is, even in some way, provincial. Further, Kant has a conflict within his thinking and it has to do with how he can claim to know what he knows. He says all kinds of things that follow from a set of categories, but the categories that he uses to explain things are categories that arise from a certain use of language. It turns out to be that if you speak a standard, average European language—for instance, the German language—Kant's categories then emerge.

But what if you spoke a different language, would you have different categories? Where does this stand? It is not clear. If you are feeling confusion, let me tell you, I am feeling confusion, too. What is Kant's standpoint? Kant also has a notion of the "I"—capital I—you say the word "I" when you say, "I think this," I say the word "I" when I think something. But Kant says this word "I" does not directly connect us with our inner selves, it is a concept we use. It is an important and convenient concept that we use. In fact, Kant makes a distinction among three things—the concept of "I" which we must use; it is part of our language, our experience of ourselves in terms of categories where we could be objects studied by a physician or by a scientist; then Kant also says, underlying all that there must be our true selves, but by the way, it is in the nature of our reason that we can't know this true self that each of us has, or each of us is.

This is peculiar. This is the odd sort of thing that happens with these strange people called philosophers. Kant is telling us that we have to ask certain questions. We can't be sure of the source of the questions. We use the word "I", but it is a concept we use and it doesn't give us a pathway to an inner true self. So we are put in a strange kind of position by Kant. What we have in Kant then is how we could be studied objectively by science, but that's an interpretation. We've got the concept of "I." We use it all the time: "I think this; I want that," but it doesn't give us knowledge of an inner reality. Then we have the notion that there must be a source of ourselves, even though we are unable truly to know it. It is, in some sense, and must remain, a mystery.

The notion of imagination is very central to Kant's philosophy. It is an important notion that he introduces and what we will need to see is that he doesn't mean the word "imagination" as we usually understand it, but this notion of imagination that we are now going to look at, has extraordinarily important implications for philosophy and for our trip together as we are exploring the journey to what we hope could be construed as the meaning of life. Because Kant says in one of his major works—he says it almost out of the blue—that all of our knowing arises from something he calls "the power of imagination." Then he says it is a blind but indispensable part of the human soul of which we are scarcely ever aware. We are supposed to use our reason. We are supposed to know, but all knowing, all use of our reason, arises from a blind but indispensable something called imagination, and this imagination is something that is the power, the energy, that drives our being.

This is a simple mystery in Kant. Let's consider it further. Let's think about it. You know, there is an old development that lives on in philosophy and it has to do with the relation between power on the one hand, and structure or forum on the other. There is a long historical tradition in which anything, even the energy of the universe, could be altogether understood rationally in terms of structure. But there is another view that says there are at least some realities and usually a candidate for one of these realities is the inner core of the self that can't be known altogether rationally, that somehow it goes beneath or beyond our rational comprehension.

Kant talks about imagination in suggestive and at the same time problematic, even unfortunate ways. What do you say about the notion that there is an energy or power deeper than our reason? That that energy or power, which is deeper than our reason, drives our understanding and that we can't use our reason to get down to it to find out its nature? But if we can't, then our knowledge is by means of reason. How does Kant even know there is such a power? As we continue our journey, what we are going to discover is that all kinds of philosophers agree with Kant that there is some blind, indispensable power at the very core of our being.

And just possibly, whatever the meaning of life is, if life has a meaning, it will have to do with our coming into touch with—our coming to be one with—whatever that deep-seated power is, and it might be non-rational. That is to say, it might be the sort of thing that is mysterious, but one thing important for us to remember is our journey; of course, that is to say, our journey along the route to the meaning of life continues. This notion of a power of some kind of energy that is the deepest element in us will continue to be part of our thinking.

The label that Kant uses is the label "imagination." As we go forward, other philosophers looking to think of ways of understanding how life is meaningful will be talking in ways very similar to Kant. They will be talking about some inner reality deeper than our reason, but they will not necessarily use the word "imagination." As we are going to see, they may use other words.

Now, the romantics for instance—and we will be thinking about the romantic tradition in a later lecture—are very caught up with this idea of an inner, irrational, perhaps even non-rational imagination. For instance, Coleridge, the English poet, will take inspiration from Kant. He will say that imagination is as important as anything can be and it is the true source of our being, the absolutely true source of our being, and it is that from which any meaning for human life must arise.

We turn to look now, reflect on, and frankly, worry about human freedom. Notice we've already discussed that Kant says that our minds are incapable of showing whether we are free or not free. What Kant says on that basis is, since we can't prove we are or we aren't free, we will just assume that we are free. He does make space in philosophy for freedom because after all, he said we can't know our true nature; therefore we couldn't know if we were free, and we can't know about freedom without falling into various contradictions. But what Kant does say, and I think is very important to consider, is that we do experience in our lives a fundamental, moral predicament and that moral predicament is that we are constantly in a battle between our sense of duty and our inclination between our rationality and our passions.

Kant has something called a "deontological" stress. It means that one is to be judged and one must judge oneself in terms of one's motives.

That is to say, it is not so important what the consequences of our actions are, what really matters is our motivation. In fact, he has ways of judging our motives. The battle is duty versus inclination; our reason versus our passion. But how can we know we have the right motives? How can we know that we are doing the right thing?

Kant offers two alternatives for evaluating motives. One alternative he offers is that you should consider whether if what you are doing, any other person should do in a similar circumstance; you should never make an exception of yourself. Another thing Kant says is that in whatever you do, you should always treat other people as ends and never use them as a means. So reflect on this for a moment. Here is Kant, and he has given us a specific, somewhat austere battleground in which to live.

You and I, I think whatever our journey is in life, wherever we hope or expect to get, whether we consider there to be or not to be a meaning in life, we probably have a rich load of experience. Kant wants to narrow it down to reason versus passion, duty against inclination; he wants to judge us all together in terms of our motives, our intentions. Are we acting out of respect for what we ought to do, something called the moral law? Or are we just looking at consequences?

By the way, in passing, something that clarifies this, something that we can get existentially anxious about if we'd like: the Internal Revenue Service has to prove intent if they think something has gone wrong. They are altogether into motives. Kant would applaud the notion that what finally matters is motive. However, medicine is something else. If the surgeon comes in—you've had your leg taken off but you were in to have your tonsils out—if the surgeon says, "I meant well; my motives were good," it probably won't work. You will probably end up suing the surgeon. You may win. We will worry a little now if there are some surgeons among us on this journey of life, no harm meant. We just want to be very clear that for Kant, it is motive that matters, the fundamental motive is respect for the moral law, to purify our will so that we don't think about consequences; we just do what we ought to do.

I think in John F. Kennedy's *Profiles in Courage*, in the preface, something like the following is said, "A person does what he or she must, regardless of personal consequences, and that is the essence of all human morality." Kant agrees. Kant agrees that that's how life ought to be lived.

Kant's views on religion are complex, significant. They give us a lot to think about. Kant has the notion of God as an absolutely necessary being. We could think of that as the god of the philosophers. It doesn't sound like a god we would bend our knee to, we would be devoted to, we would worship. Kant has an abstract philosophical notion of an absolutely necessary being. He says that you and I along the journey of life can't help but think about whether there is such a being. We can't know, but if we think as philosophical people, we will think that, yes, we have to reflect further on this, and it is Kant's view that as we reflect further on the notion of an absolutely necessary being, there are no proofs that work, no proofs that this absolutely necessary being exists.

Kant himself, the person, is very wrapped up in what could be called "teleological" concerns. That is, he sees a kind of purposiveness in nature. He doesn't think you could prove it is there, but he has a sense that there is a kind of purposiveness in nature, and though he says proofs for a philosophical god, an absolutely necessary being don't work, he has intimations through this sense of design, which he says you couldn't prove is there. But he has intimations that that tells us something about a powerful being beyond us.

How Kant actually works off his religious views for you and me, how he would construe religion related to us on the journey toward the meaning of life, is extraordinary. He thinks that religion must be understood thoroughly and rationally. We have to have a thoroughly rational conception of the religious life. We must not let our feelings be indulged. We must work thoroughly from within reason and from in the moral life. Kant claims to come up with an argument that would show that we are immortal. That argument goes as follows. We have the duty, which we would experience if we closely examined our inner lives to perfect ourselves.

Kant claims that you could only have the strong sense of duty, which he says any of us would have if we concentrated on our inner moral life. You could only have that sense of duty if you were in fact able to discharge that duty. So, if we have this sense of duty—Kant claimed he did at least—to reach perfection, then we must be able to become perfect, and by perfect, he means completely moral, doing everything out of duty. Oh dear! What Kant tells us is that it is obvious to him, it should be obvious to you and me, that in a finite period of time, that is the period of time allotted to us in this life, we couldn't perfect ourselves. But if we have that duty, and anything that we have a duty to do, we could, Kant says therefore there must be an infinite period of time available to us. If we have the duty and we can discharge it, you and I can become perfect, but we can't in this world; then we must live long enough that that perfection could be achieved.

Many philosophers looked at Kant, looked at his writings, saw the kind of genius he was and said, "But this doesn't add up. This is almost a crazy notion. Do we really have the obligation on ourselves to perfect ourselves? Does that mean even if we had that obligation, that we could? Could that really mean we would live forever in order to become perfect?" And Kant even adds to this. Kant even says, "Well, there must be a God because after all, if you were perfect, then you should be rewarded with a complete happiness, and only an extraordinarily powerful being could give the kind of happiness you deserved if you became perfect." So it doesn't prove it, but there is something to the logic of moral life that suggests that God exists as the basis for rewarding us, rewarding us for having become perfect— that is, morally pure—and we can do it. This is extraordinary. This is an extraordinary set of doctrines and the reactions to them are many, and many are even outraged by them. But this is the kind of confidence that Kant has.

Let us move a little now toward a conclusion. Let us consider further these strange things that we've looked at. We've looked at a rational conception of human life. We have looked at the notion that we cannot really know our true nature. Kant tells us that nonetheless, we can look within ourselves and discover duty, and the need for duty to fight desire, duty to fight inclination, reason to fight passion, and that we even can see that we have the duty to completely perfect ourselves along those lines.

This is a very stern view. This is a very austere view. It is a view that puzzles some; it outrages others. But especially it is austerity—the notion that reason would be caught up with moral duty and that religion would arise out of a rational conception of moral duty— virtually unhinged or at least created an immensely strong reaction in a number of philosophers, particularly a group which we now call "Romantics," and it is the romantic reaction to Kant's rationalism that we will be looking at in our next lecture, in our next time together along the journey for determining whether there is a meaning to life.

Lecture Four
Kant and the Romantic Reaction

Scope:

Kant becomes subject to much criticism for comprehending the trajectory and ideal of human life too restrictively as a battle between moral duty and personal inclination. Especially unacceptable to his *Romantic* critics is his description of passions as "Cancers of our Pure Reason." In reaction, a philosophical agenda emerges that glorifies the individual and the exceptional—a movement that we now call *Romanticism*. This movement stresses intuitive capacities and the promise of genius. It also emphasizes the power of nature and of communal life, set apart from the rest of society, to heal human wounds and to enhance human potential by lifting it out of the tediously ordinary and away from the idea of the moral construed as the regimented and merely moralistic. Romanticism tends to vacillate between extolling those rare cases of creative genius and treasuring the ("romanticized") life of the simple person who is removed from the chronic stressfulness of business and industry.

Outline

I. We have seen how Kant advocates a strict moral life in the face of our ultimate human ignorance regarding the true nature of things. But Kant also leaves us with the dilemmas of the unknown, the external world as it is in itself and our own (true, but shrouded) inner nature.

    A. "The unknown thing as it is in itself" is sometimes referred to (quite problematically) as the *noumenal* world.

        1. The interpretive and inherently conflicted—dialectical—features of human reason prevent us from grasping things as they are in themselves.

        2. The consequence of the success of the historical movement called Nominalism was that reality came to be viewed as comprising individual items. In Kant, however, our human understanding works only in a classificatory way, in terms of categories. Thus, we cannot directly know the reality of individual items, according to Kant.

3. The notion of a noumenal world is even more problematic: What is suggested is a reality arrived at through the very thinking of it. In addition or alternatively, reality is altogether nonsensible, unavailable to our normal and accepted modes of encounter, and thus otherworldly in nature.

4. Unavoidably, a sense of separation and even of alienation grow. Science gets construed as telling us more and more about the appearances of things to us, but reality, thereby, remains shrouded—unattainable by and unavailable to us.

5. Fideism—a leap of faith regarding the nature of reality—is tempting, but the Enlightenment's, and especially Kant's own reliance on reason, makes blind, nonrational faith no legitimate alternative.

B. Kant even considered our own (true, but hidden) inner natures as potentially driven by reason.

1. Kant divides our inner lives into *duties* and *inclinations*. The passions—a word that encompasses a wide swath of ordinary human desires—are viewed by Kant as *cancers of human reason.*

2. The German philosopher Johann Fichte, claiming to be Kant's true successor, viewed the world as a moral testing ground.

3. Kant does claim to discover a sublimity *within*, something occasionally encountered through a fusion of imagination and understanding, but one that lies beyond images and concepts.

4. In his doctrine of autonomy, Kant demands a separation of desire from will, a separation that provokes a strong reaction from proponents of the Romantic Movement.

5. Inconsistently, Kant suggests that we do have a possible access to our true natures through a particular phenomenon (in German an *Uhrphenomenon*): the will.

II. What we have come in retrospect to think of as Romanticism grows out of an intense desire to experience the unity of personhood, to transcend dichotomies, both in oneself and (possibly) in relation to others, and thereby to come into direct contact with reality itself, something masked by the worlds of ordinary experience and science. A fusion is sought.

- **A.** The aesthetic experience is taken as paradigmatic, for it arises out of feeling and gives further rise to feelings of unity, unification, and of belonging. Through this experience, a number of problems are solved simultaneously.

    1. One example is the opposition between mechanism and teleology.

    2. Another is the division of the person into separate and warring components.

    3. Further dichotomies are resolved through the opening of an avenue, a potentially healing one, to a religious experience that is not conditioned by science, morality, or general belief systems.

- **B.** Through the work of Fichte and Johann Gottfried von Herder, a German Romantic philosopher, the normative notion arises of unity of a people in terms of shared features of their language and culture.

    1. In Fichte, this notion has a strong voluntaristic and nationalistic tone that will clash with the more cosmopolitan and universalist aspects of Enlightenment thinking.

    2. In Herder, cultural elements get greater play, and unities of culture are celebrated.

    3. These celebrations of variety and individuating differences fly in the face of a uniformity implied by nonconformity coming from Enlightenment values.

III. Largely congruent with these Romantic motifs and urgings, an expressionistic understanding of the Self and (particularly) of language emerges. Expression itself is believed to offer the means of coming into touch with one's underlying (true) Self and thereby enabling one to become authentically individual.

- **A.** The agony of Romantic individualism is that it may be a great—and even noble—but failed attempt to establish a deep unity within the life of the individual.

    1. It attempted to convey ideas and ideals through artistic and nonrational means alone.

2. It construed the artist not only as an outsider but as the paradigm of individuality.

3. It was especially concerned with the quality versus quantity of life.

4. Romanticism involved a quandary regarding rights. Were they primarily political, having to do with the establishment of organic communities, or were they more psychological, having to do with inner integrity.

5. The Romantic Movement rejected Realism because of its concern with calculation, external success, and worldly power.

B. Some core values and conflicts within Romanticism have lingered long after the movement waned.

1. The notion of the *lonely wanderer* emerges as a successor to the otherworldly directed axial pilgrim.

2. A special valuation is given to that which lies deeply within.

3. Conflicted reactions emerge regarding communities and cosmopolitanism. Thus, the simple and the "untainted" are given the highest value.

4. The Romantics knew that beyond organization, industrialization, urbanization, and bureaucracy, there must be something with which to connect, but the challenge was to find the true inner Self.

Essential Reading:

Isaiah Berlin, *The Roots of Romanticism*.

W. T. Jones, *The Romantic Syndrome: Toward a New Method in Cultural Anthropology and History of Ideas*.

Supplementary Reading:

James Engell, *The Creative Imagination: Enlightenment to Romanticism*.

Questions to Consider:

1. What are some of the central values of the Romantics?

2. What are some of the core problems that the Romantics sought to address?

3. What limitations do you see in the Romantic outlook?

Lecture Four—Transcript

Kant and the Romantic Reaction

In our journey together to see how some philosophers have understood the quest for the meaning of life, we just looked at a very rational account—that is, Kant's account. I should say right now that if it makes perfect sense to you, and Kant's account fits together and seems perfectly rational, and you are even driven to accept it or take it very seriously and want to believe it, perhaps I didn't give the kind of lecture I should, because, after Kant, countless philosophers take issue with Kant. They do not believe that what he says or all parts of it add up.

At the same time, we've seen in Kant glimpses of some kind of a mystery. Kant uses the word "imagination"; maybe it wasn't the right label for an underlying energy that is part of our nature that is beneath our reason. But we have glimpsed in Kant the elements of a mystery that perhaps we can't quite reach rationally. One thing is sure. Kant's account of reason is very austere. It motivates his account of the moral life. He even accounts for religion in this very rational way.

There are very strong reactions to this, and one of them is referred to as "Romanticism." Romanticism thinks that this Kantian notion is too rational, too austere and confining. They think that the strict adherence to a rigid moral conception of life primps us and that it leaves us with certain dilemmas. It leaves us with dilemmas that we have to look into. Let us consider on the one hand, there is the unknown. We can't know the true nature of reality; we can't know our inner nature and its ultimate being; we can't know how the external world is in itself, only the ways that science can grasp it. At the same time, there are things shrouded from us. There are things that are beneath our rational capacity to grasp.

One, which is beyond us, Kant construes as the *noumenal* world. What does Kant mean by a noumenal world? Well, he says we can only interpret so we couldn't know by our reason what this noumenal world is like. Kant says whatever this noumenal world is like, perhaps God, if there is a God, could know that noumenal world simply by thinking it. But Kant also says, and let's consider this further, that our human way of encountering things is by means of our senses, and if there is a noumenal world, that noumenal world might be the kind of reality that is beyond what our senses can tell us. Well, then, where are we?

Problems are made even more difficult because of something called *nominalism*. Kant is an inheritor of nominalism. Nominalism is the view that each and every thing, whether a noumenal something that may be beyond our senses, or any particular thing, is an individual. It is not a type. But Kant claims that we can only know by means of categories. Whatever we encounter, we can't know what we encounter in its specific individuality. We can only know it by means of the categories that we have at our disposable. And therefore, in that sense, our reason is also limited.

Kant further claims that we have intimations. Let's consider this claim a little bit further—intimations of a world beyond this one that might altogether escape our senses. But he also says that we are sense bound. We can only know what we encounter and what we encounter, we can only know by means of our senses and what they can interpret, and there may be things that fall outside of the net of our senses.

Kant is a great believer in science. Science structures are experience and it tells us about the appearance of things, but it doesn't give us the reality behind the appearance of things. The reality behind the appearance of things remains shrouded in mystery. What would you do then? Where would we go from here? One view is called "Fideism". Fideism suggests that maybe there could be a leap of faith regarding the nature of reality. Whether there is a noumenal reality that's beyond our senses or not, whether there is an ultimate reality that reason can or couldn't get, perhaps a great leap of faith might draw us to that, but Kant doesn't allow that. Kant doesn't allow such a leap of faith because all faith must grow out of reason. It must be rational. It must be a moral faith that is structured rationally. Only then would we be led to perhaps a religion.

As we saw in our last lecture, Kant's notion of the journey of life involves duties and inclinations, and if there is a journey to life, it is meant to be the victory of duty over inclination, but think about it. Let's think about our lives. Aren't our lives a lot more than just duty and inclination? Don't we have a great bunch of desires, feelings and emotions? Kant inclines to call everything that isn't rational moral duty a "cancer of human reason." He tends to talk as if that dimension of our life that isn't purely rational is in some way cancerous, and to be overcome that insofar as we don't act out of rational duty, we have somehow failed.

A late 18th/early 19th century philosopher, Johann Fichte, following in the course of Kant, thinks that perhaps we should view this world as a moral testing ground, a place where we learn how always to act in accordance with duty, never in accordance with inclination, and if we understand why we are in this world, we are in this world to perfect ourselves, Fichte would say, "And the world is there as a battleground through which we would reach moral perfection."

Kant says some other odd things as well. Kant says that sometimes our imagination—again, that mysterious force—fuses and wells up and connects with our reason and understanding, and when it does that, we have some experience of sublimity. We have some experience of something we can't articulate that elevates us that we do not experience as thoroughly rational, that we can't fully comprehend. In some way in the face of everything Kant and even Fichte say about duty, that sense of sublimity, at least in Kant, gives us a kind of sense of transcendence.

Kant also talks about autonomy—autonomy as always acting as your own person, never in the kind of prison of what your desires are tugging at you to do. When the Romantics hear about this notion of autonomy, always asking and asking and asking and working in terms of moral categories and not understanding life of terms of desires, they in fact are outraged by that. They are outraged by the notion that feeling, emotion and desire aren't allowed to carry any day.

Similarly, they are very caught up in the notion that there are sublime experiences possible. We get glimpses of something that's beyond what our reason and our sense of duty can ever give to us. Out of that, Romanticism begins to arise. Glimpsing at Kant's notion of possible sublimity, glimpsing also at Kant's notion that when you come down to it, there is autonomy, but to the Romantics, the fact that there is autonomy means maybe we are pulling ourselves back and not embracing our full being.

Kant has one other thing to say before we move now beyond him. There is a strange notion that is picked up by later philosophers. It is controversial to some extent to the degree to which it fully isn't Kant. It is the notion of the *Uhrphenomenon* as some basic underlying phenomenon in our experience, a phenomenon that is within us. Perhaps it is connected with our will, perhaps it is connected with our imagination, but whatever it is connected with, Kant sometimes talks as if in the midst of all his rationalism, there may just be a way that we can come into touch within ourselves to a kind of ultimate reality.

So there, Kant has opened the door, but he has not allowed even himself through it. He has talked about imagination and sublimity, and he talks about autonomy and the victory of duty over inclination in a way that enrages and causes reaction in this group of philosophers that we call "Romantics."

What Romanticism arises out of is the intense desire to experience the unity of personhood, to transcend dichotomies, both in ourselves and in others, and to come into some kind of direct contact with reality itself, something that might be masked by the worlds of ordinary experience and science. Some kind of fusion is sought. The Romantics have the underlying idea that we separate ourselves out too much, that too much of our experience does not have a kind of fusion and focus to it. These same Romantics believe that what we need is to look toward the creative, the artistic—the aesthetic. That is taken as the paradigm, as something that Kant almost opened the door to with this notion of the sublime or the imagination, but didn't let us through, and if we could just be more attuned to the aesthetic, that would give us the sense of unity, of unification and belonging.

It is part of the Romantic idea that we long for a belonging, a place that we can find to be home and that that is an underlying thing we want. For the Romantics, the reliance on reason is too austere and it doesn't give us that full significant sense of being one with ourselves, and having a sense that we are at home with ourselves and at home with and in the world. They are desperately concerned— these Romantics are—to find some way to get beyond the opposition between mechanism and teleology. The notion is that the world could be viewed as a big machine and yet the intimation we always have that there is some kind of purpose, some kind of sense of direction to the world, even if science often looks at it as a machine.

Also, these same Romantics are concerned about the division of the person into separate and warring components—reason and desire, public and private self, reason and passion, your will fighting your emotions. What the Romantics hope for is some fuse and fusing experience that will give us a sense of oneness, a sense of connection with some kind of a whole. They also look in a very problematic way at the religious. They wonder if there might be some kind of religious experience, clearly for them, not institutional, nor formal and doctrinal, but some kind of experience beyond general belief systems that could somehow make us whole and give us a sense of fusion with something beyond a wholeness that would make us feel at home, that the journey of life brought us to the proper belonging and that our longing for a belonging would be taking care of.

Two philosophers—Johann Fichte, who I've just mentioned, and Johann Herder, who I mention now—pick up in certain ways on some of these Romantic notions. Take the case of Fichte. You get the notion of the unity of a people. Now, this isn't even just the notion of an individual. In Fichte, it is the notion that in some way a nation can almost be a person. It is a strong voluntaristic notion that there are particular people. This goes against cosmopolitan understanding. It is the Universalist conception the Enlightenment has that fundamentally we are all the same. Fichte picks up on the notion that there are different kinds of people, nations for example and that they have special traits.

Johann Herder, who lived as Fichte did, at the end of the 18th century, also thought that cultures differed. That is, there are differing cultures and how you are enmeshed or embedded in a particular culture that might go way beyond rational conception, which that may go way beyond a kind of uniformity. That in the depths of a particular national tradition, with its language and its culture, may very well be found a way to fuse with oneself, with other people, and with a larger world that reason maybe only dissects, reason maybe only categorizes.

Very much part of what we've been talking about in this Romantic motif—this notion of the journey of life as a longing for a belonging, a longing to be one with oneself, a longing to fuse with something beyond—very much part of that is a kind of expressionistic understanding of the self, and out of that, a special emphasis is given to language. Expression is believed to offer the means of coming to the underlying unity with oneself. To find out who you really are, you must find a way to express yourself, and if you express yourself and find the right way to do it, you will come to be who you truly are.

There is agony in this notion. There is agony in this Romantic tradition, and it is the agony that it may be a great and noble idea, but in some ways, perhaps it fails. It fails to establish a deep unity within the individual. We have to look for a moment at whether there is this kind of failure. If Kant was too rational—and the reaction was to find the wholeness of the person, to find a way of a belonging that went beyond rational distinctions—then what about this reaction? Well, it attempted to convey ideas and ideals through artistic and non-rational means alone.

Let me pause for a moment about this because the next reflection is one we will want to stay with. It will keep coming up in our time together. What we get out of the Romantics is the notion of the outsider. The outsider comes to be viewed as the paradigm of the individual. This outsider was construed as someone who did not usually connect with the normal ordinary world. People who are not outsiders—insiders—are viewed as getting reassurance, support. They are viewed as getting security through their connections with other people. Yes, as I told you, Fichte did say that it is the nation that mattered, and Herder did say that it was a culture and a language that mattered, but the underlying drama and drive of the Romantics was the notion that there would be individuals; they would be outsiders. As outsiders without the support, the security, the reassurance of community and society, these outsiders would be vulnerable and their very vulnerability might make them more in touch with realities that reason wouldn't reach, and it might open them up to a kind of creativity that they might not otherwise have.

Kant was concerned with a scientific community of investigation. He had a rational faith and a moral life. The Romantics tend to be much more concerned about individuals. Yes, language. Yes, culture. Yes, nations. But really, individuals—vulnerable individuals who, as outsiders, do not connect—do not connect in a way that offers reassurance and that failure to connect opens them and makes them vulnerable—vulnerable in a way that makes them touch more closely to themselves and perhaps releases a creative power.

Well, what becomes fundamental is a concern for the distinction between the quality of life and the quantity of life for these Romantics. It is not how long you live; it is the quality of your life, whether that life can be a creative one, whether you can allow yourself vulnerability. Yes, there may be reason, but perhaps reason doesn't hit deep enough into who we truly are. Perhaps reason, in all its rationality, can't reach far enough, far enough beyond, into the ultimate nature of things, and if Kant is right that reason can't do that, so be it. Maybe the vulnerable individual outsider, the person who has had this glimmer of the sublime, this experience of the creative, maybe it is that individual that can do this.

These same Romantics are very, very concerned and have quandaries about what our rights are. There is a lot of talk about rights. Should you construe rights as political ones? Many of the Romantics thought that you should have the right to overthrow the way things are if it is discriminatory, stale, conventional, restrictive of creative powers. Many of these Romantics thought you should have the right to form small communities and be left alone to do as you would do. But at that same time, these same Romantics thought that there was another sense of light. We could almost call it a psychological sense of right. Whether community or not, whether the right to change the world if it doesn't speak to the human heart, there was also this notion that you could only have an inner integrity; you could only truly be an individual if you are left alone to be an individual. and the right not to be interfered with came to be construed as a very important right for these same Romantics.

They rejected what we would call "realism". They saw it as too hard headed. It was trying to quantify the agonies of the heart; it was too much concern with calculation, with external success, with worldly power. The Romantics thought that the conventional world, however successful in ordinary terms it could make you, was a world which nonetheless could erode your potential, could gradually bring into your life staleness. Some of these core values of Romanticism stress on the individual, stress on the notion of the creative and the imaginative. They linger long after Romanticism.

Frankly, often we review these Romantic values as adolescent. We actually do. It is a fact that we often say that these Romantic tendencies are fine if you are young, but as you grow up, as you become mature, you have to abandon them. You have to become more rational. You have to become more practical, but the Romantic idea is becoming practical, becoming more conventional, even in worldly terms, "successful" might be at the cost of your inner integrity. It might be at the cost of your potential creativity, and if it is so, in the extreme Romantic position, it is better not to succeed in a worldly sense, if through the Romantic life: the Romantic life of coming to find a way to express yourself, and become one with yourself, if through that route, you can have some inner sense of integrity.

These Romantics do not have an enlightenment notion of a universal community. They tend to stress the notion of the lonely wanderer who emerges then as the successor to what I've called so far, the other worldly directed "axial pilgrim". Let's pause here for a moment. Think about this. The axial model that we've looked at is: life would be a journey, and a journey from here to an elsewhere. The elsewhere would be the place of our true belonging. The journey then would liberate us. It might even be an historical journey, but whatever kind of journey, we'd go from where we are to an elsewhere where we would belong, where we would find a home. We've seen that for Kant that might be reached rationally, even in the face of Kant's restriction of reason.

But what you get with the Romantics is that maybe you have a home deep within you, in terms of your creative abilities, but perhaps you will always have to be a wanderer, maybe always a lonely wanderer. Maybe though you are in, you are not of this world and your true home will never be found—that however creative, however much you go against convention, you may always wander. Therefore, there may be, in the face of the quest for creativity, no final home that would be found.

Conflicted reactions emerge regarding communities and the cosmopolitan in these Romantics. They are very, very concerned that if we become more and more like each other, we may communicate better, but at the same time, we will become unfortunately more uniform, more like each other. They are very concerned that we do not get trapped by sophistication, that we not get trapped by the notion that a great deal of knowledge of various parts of the world, and a great education that knows many things. They are concerned that that might take us away from the very simplicity of the inner life, and if we are taken away from that simplicity of the inner life, have we perhaps lost our own souls?

So as you can see, these Romantics themselves are conflicted. They know that reason has limitation. They know that there is something wrong with a life in which duty is put against desire. They know there is something wrong with a life where we have to put on a public face and our private world is somehow something that can't be unified with our public being. They have a sense sometimes that maybe beyond urbanization, beyond industrialization, beyond organization and beyond bureaucracy, there may be something that one could connect with, but their journey seems to them agonizing, at times futile. But they have this sense that we have to have the integrity, we have to accept the challenge of trying to find that inner self, and that perhaps if we find more ways to express ourselves, more ways to find an authenticity that may require that we pull back from the world, the better chance we have to find our souls and perhaps even to heal our souls.

So we have two problems, don't we? We have rationalism in Kant that seems limited, and if that is the journey of life, doesn't it seem austere? What about the Romantics? They speak of so many different things, things that seem to offer hope—creativity, imagination, pulling back from the crowd—but at the same time, we don't know how to make those things fit together.

If you will think about it, as we are taking our journey together, we have said very little about history. Kant has a view that says little about historical development. We just affirm reason. The Romantics are concerned to rebel, to step back, to get beyond or beneath reason, but never with a sense of historical development, as if there could be an historical pathway we might take.

What we are going to look at when we are together again as we pursue this journey is how history may work in this regard, because the next philosopher we are going to consider is Hegel. Hegel, who lived from 1770 to 1831, had a very strong sense of how Kant could be right about reason and the Romantics could be right about passion, but they could be brought together if we understood what the true development of history is.

Lecture Five
Hegel on the Human Spirit

Scope:

The Enlightenment and its consummate philosopher, Immanuel Kant, pay little attention to human history. Their focus is on the future as a place where—through reason, science, and education—the harm caused by tradition and superstition can be overcome and equality achieved among people. Georg Wilhelm Friedrich Hegel (1770–1831) dramatically alters this picture of human life and seeks to undermine its assumptions. Attesting to our unity as human beings, he construes us most fundamentally as Spirit, and not as reason and will, or duty and inclination. As Spirit, we participate in and even constitute a process. Properly approached, the meaning of our lives can be found through this ongoing process. Hegel provides a blueprint for understanding human history as the unfolding of Spirit—in effect, as God's autobiography and the only way to comprehend divinity after the advances of science and the liberating doctrines of the Enlightenment. He provides models for meaningful and even exceptional human lives.

Outline

I. Georg W. F. Hegel is one of the extraordinary figures in the history of philosophy and his understanding of our human situation, even in our pervasive rejection of it, determines much of our philosophical self-understanding and sense of how to guide our lives today.

II. What are the influential pre-Hegelian accounts of history and in their terms what is history's actual purpose?

A. History can be understood as *cyclical*, both in "wisdom" literature and in Plato.

1. The notion of a detached escape from history is a controversial one.

2. Dimensions of the axial attitude are found in both cyclical accounts, as well as in reincarnation theory.

B. A brief elaboration of history with reference to guides will be helpful.

1. The influence of the Platonic journey from the Cave is an important one.

2. For a better understanding, we might also mention Socratic, Stoical, Messianic, and "Eastern" models of deliverance from history.

III. What is to be made of Hegel's influential account of the development of history, involving the notion of Spirit?

   A. Hegel's understanding of human life is best comprehended through the notion of Spirit.

      1. Spirit (in German, *Geist*) must be understood as a process, not as an object.

      2. Construing ourselves as *consciousness* or *mind* can be misleading.

      3. Hegel's notion of Spirit is a fusion of reason and imagination. In Kant, these would have been separated elements.

      4. Spirit in Hegel is a totality, rather than an exclusively cognitive capacity.

   B. Spirit has a problematic reflexivity in that it bears a relation to itself, the nature and quality of which is essential to its constitution.

      1. Hegel articulates this reflexiveness in terms of the categories "in-itself" and "for-itself."

      2. Hegel describes components that enter into selfhood, as well as their possible separations and conflicts.

   C. Spirit—construed now as the *Self*—invariably experiences itself in a mediated manner. Our consciousness of ourselves always reflects those situations in which we find ourselves.

      1. Notions of Spirit in Medieval life and Romanticism provide examples of such mediation.

      2. There are intimations that mediation can be transcended in Hegel's account of Absolute Spirit. But the distinction between belief and pure insight discourages such a thing.

   D. Hegel's concept of *Absolute Spirit* has a problematic relation to our individual and finite spirits.

1. Absolute Spirit is a successor notion to the notion of God and involves an understanding of history's unfolding as God's own autobiography.
2. History is sometimes taken as a means and measure of the justification of particular historical actions and events.
   a. This view can be highly problematic.
   b. We have to separate moral from creative activities.
3. Hegel claims that Spirit develops over historical time in a manner that he refers to as *dialectical*.
   a. Hegel has an understanding of rational discrepancy that has a significant relation to both Plato and Kant's notions of discrepancy.
   b. In Hegel's *Phenomenology of Spirit* (1907), we find a distinction between existential discrepancy and rational discrepancy.
   c. Hegel writes about socioeconomic forces and their collision. Such collision constitutes a dialectic working itself out in concrete history.
4. Hegel understands history to have reached an end.
   a. The end of history signifies the closure of the possibility of anything genuinely new happening, not the stoppage of history as a set of occurrences.
   b. This notion involves *Aufhebung*, a German term that is virtually untranslatable. That is, we live through the conflicts of history. We do not abandon a conflicting element; we absorb it.

IV. Hegel places great emphasis on the role of great people in the configuring of history.

A. Certain people are construed as the embodiment and expression of ideas that move history forward to its next stage of development.

1. Hegel insists that ideas are the prime movers of history.
2. In the course of working in reason's service, we can be deceived by reason itself. This deception Hegel calls the *Cunning of Reason*.

B. Hegel has a positive conception of the statesman or leader who creates or sustains a stable context in which the life of Spirit can flourish.

    1. Hegel claims that the rights we possess and the duties that we have to the state are intimately connected.

    2. Hegel has more appreciation for an activist state involved in culture than in a state that acts like a neutral umpire.

C. Hegel has a notion of the philosopher.

    1. Philosophy is the highest of human possibilities.

    2. Influenced by Johann Wolfgang von Goethe, Hegel believes that all experience must be appropriated. This belief is an alternative, both to the spectatorial standpoint of the Greeks, and to the ecstatic standpoint found in much religion.

V. Individual human life in community and the creative development of the life of Spirit are in tension with each other in Hegel.

A. Formal morality and a life led in terms of concretely embedded customs offer different models for living.

    1. Kant's deontological formalism is viewed by Hegel as empty and motivationally sterile.

    2. Customary behavior within the norms of a specific community cannot help at times but raise serious problems for a community member.

B. Moral evaluation may take place on a different scale than that which serves as a measure of creative output.

    1. Ludwig von Beethoven, Pablo Picasso, and James Joyce serve as helpful, illustrative examples of split verdicts.

    2. Invariably, a conflict exists between progress and conservation, between creativity and formal moral customs.

VI. Hegel has problems resolving the tensions between aspiring to greatness and living out an ordinary existence.

A. Hegel finds the dynamics of dominance and subordination endemic to human life.

1. Hegel emphasizes passion and extraordinary acts of will.
2. Hegel gives great significance to recognition. To be fully human, we must be recognized by others as human.

B. Hegel trumpets many rewards through an ordinary life lived out in a stable and culturally rich society.

C. Hegel says that we *can* tell a story about human history, that both wonderful and terrible events have happened in this history, and that history enables us to relive the great moments of history.

Essential Reading:

Walter Kaufmann, *Hegel.*

Terry Pinkard, *Hegel's Phenomenology: The Sociality of Reason.*

Supplementary Reading:

Georg Wilhelm Friedrich Hegel, *Phenomenology of Spirit.*

Robert Pippin, *Hegel's Idealism: The Satisfactions of Self-Consciousness.*

Questions to Consider:

1. Why does Hegel understand our human nature as Spirit?
2. What is the relationship among history, religion, and the unfolding of Spirit?

Lecture Five—Transcript
Hegel on the Human Spirit

We looked at both rational accounts of the journey toward the meaning of life and non-rational accounts—Kant, a rational account; the Romantics in differing ways, not so rational accounts, maybe non-rational ones. But each gives us a kind of guidance and neither talks a lot about history. The philosopher we will look at now is Georg Wilhelm Friedrich Hegel and how he talks about the role of history in human life.

Hegel is probably one of the most extraordinary figures in the history of philosophy. His understanding of our human situation, even if we pervasively reject it, determines much of our philosophical understanding and sense of how to guide our lives, even today. Very much we live in the aftermath of Hegel and his sense of history. What were some of the influential pre-Hegelian accounts of history, and in their terms, what was history's actual purpose?

One account would view history as cyclical. History is just recurring, recurring and recurring. In the Hebrew Bible, we have the *Book of Ecclesiastics*. It says there is nothing new under the sun, things just keep happening in a kind of cycle. The Greeks also had a notion of history as cycle, and that suggested—it is also found in parts of the philosopher Plato—that what we need is an escape from history. That is a controversial notion—that we could go beyond or above history and no longer be caught, trapped, by its cycles. If you think of the axial attitude, that life is a journey from here to an elsewhere, that axial attitude is even found in some of the cyclical accounts and it is also found in reincarnation theory. If we do a brief account of history, with reference to guides who have perhaps suggested that we get beyond history, it might help us.

There is the view, which we find in Plato, that what we have to do is get out of the cave of ignorance and be guided beyond shadows, appearances and an experience of things that are confusing to us to a bright daylight. We might also mention Socrates—of course, one of the great figures of Western philosophy—who saw philosophy as learning how to die, as escaping the body, as leaving the prison of the body and finding an elsewhere that is beyond the recurrent events that happen in history.

There is also the Stoic notion. It has many forms, but one of its norms and forms is that whether history is cyclical or going someplace, history is dangerous and it is best that we detach ourselves from it. We do not get involved in it. We take a step back. If the Romantics thought that the industrial, urban, conventional world was something to get away from to discover imagination and creativity, the Stoics thought that the whole world was problematic in terms of the things that happened in it, things that could spin out of control, destructive things. Some of these Stoics counseled a detachment that we would step back from what was happening in history.

There are also Messianic notions. They are more linear that a Messiah figure, an anointed one would come and lead us beyond the travails of history, and many religious people hold strongly to that view. There are also Eastern mystical notions, notions that we could be delivered through meditation from history and either deep within us or in another kind of dimension, experience peace.

What could be made of Hegel's very influential account of the development of history? It involves the notion of spirit, which is a new notion for us to consider in our journey to try to understand whether there could be, from a philosophical standpoint, a meaning to life. Hegel understands us, what we are as human beings in terms of spirit. Now in German, the word spirit is *Geist*, and it is so hard to get translated properly into our language of English, because "spirit" is not spirits as in something you might drink, or spirit as in ghosts, for Hegel's spirit is a fundamental energy that we have. It is a fusion of elements in us. Think of spirit for Hegel as a process, a process that is us, that we undergo, that drives us forward.

Hegel was very, very reluctant to think of human beings as a consciousness or a mind. It sounds so mental. It makes us sound like spectators. What Hegel thought was that that would be misleading, because if you understand spirit as dynamic energy, that is really what we are, and Hegel understood that dynamic energy. If we were to explain it in Kant's terms, we could describe it as a fusion of reason and imagination, but Hegel didn't want to say reason and imagination. What he wanted to say was "spirit" and that spirit was a fundamental unity; that it is, will always be, a totality, that it is never just a cognitive capacity.

The Greeks in much of Western philosophy thought, "Oh, the journey of life was simply to know." Hegel thought that knowing was important, but there was a lot more than knowing involved in the journey of living. Knowing was important to the discovery of the meaning of life, but it wasn't the full story. Hegel says that our spirit, which is what we are, has a problematic reflexivity to it. Pause with me now. We have to get this clear because this is an important notion—not completely easy, but we can get it—that we are not just a something, like an apple is an apple, or a rock is a rock; we as people relate to ourselves. We have a relation to ourselves, and that relation we have to ourselves is just as much us as the self we relate to.

He articulated this in terms of categories of in itself and for itself. We are who we are, but we also have experiences, perceptions and images of ourselves, and these images we have of ourselves, these conceptions, are just as much a part of who we are as the self, that we are that we have conceptions about. There is me, there is how I see me. These can be in conflict, but me, and how I see me—you and how you see yourself—that also is who and what you are, even if you and I and how we see ourselves are in conflict with each other.

Hegel adds to this complex situation when he says that the way we relate to ourselves is in what he calls a "mediated" manner. It is not just that I have a direct relation to myself; my relation to myself is embedded in the world and the experiences in which I am involved. It is embedded in culture. It is embedded in political situations. I don't just relate to myself in a vacuum. For instance, think of medieval people. They not only were people, they sustained certain kinds of relations to themselves, but it was a medieval world they lived in, so their relation that they understood themselves to have with themselves, had medieval clothing to it.

Take the Romantics. The Romantics just simply weren't the specific, separate, creative individuals that they were. They also had a relation with themselves through which they understood themselves, and that relation took place in—yes, you guessed it—a Romantic environment of being an outsider, of being creative, of getting glimpses of perhaps some deep reality within or mysterious reality beyond. That entered into how they related to themselves and related intimately.

There are intimations of Hegel, but they are only intimations that maybe you could transcend the context, the environment in which you found yourself related to yourself. But he talks on the one hand about belief; on the other side, a special insight. As he untangles the notions of what we believe about ourselves and possibly a separate special insight we get about ourselves, he decides that we couldn't finally, when all is said and done, have a relation to ourselves that didn't find itself embedded in circumstances. You see, I couldn't be me, the same me in a Romantic world as in the medieval world, and none of us, on the journey of life, can be anything other than we are in the world in which we find ourselves.

But now, as Hegel spins this out, as Hegel says we relate to ourselves, we relate to ourselves in a context and the context is an historical one, there are problems. He has the notion of absolute spirit. Not your spirit, my spirit, along the journey of life, but an absolute spirit, and that is his successor notion to God. Hegel understands God as being the unfolding of human history. Therefore, he understands God as history itself, and he understands the unfolding of history as God's autobiography. Now, this is very difficult because awful things happen in history. At any time you listen to me, at any time you look around, terrible things are happening. If history is God's autobiography, how do you explain that these terrible things are happening? This is a deep problem for Hegel. It is very highly problematic.

Let's consider. Let's consider very closely. History is God's autobiography, but awful things happen in history. What does that tell us about God? What does it tell us about reality? One thing we are told is that we have to separate moral from creative activities. Maybe awful things happen in history, but in the course of these awful things happening in history, maybe creative consequences arise. Maybe there are extraordinary triumphs for the human spirit. One could say for example, "Look at a wonderful cathedral." We don't pay attention to the fact that countless people may have suffered. Maybe they worked beyond their capacities to build the cathedral. We just are taken by the fact that, well, there it is. There is the result. Maybe then we could understand history as having a creative meaning, even though from a moral standpoint, some bad things happen.

Hegel also tells us that spirit develops over historical time in a manner that he calls "dialectical". He says if you look at history, it is a set of conflicts. There are things in history that don't add up. Plato says they don't add up at a high level and that if we look at the furthest point of our reason, we can see ways in which things don't make full sense. Kant says—we've already talked about this in our journey—that reason just simply can't, without contradiction, let us know how things really are. But Hegel's notion of dialectic is different. You and I on the journey of life—and he talks about this in the phenomenology of spirit—are very much caught up in conflicts. If history is God's autobiography, if history is the history of God's consciousness, then we have to realize that not only are individual lives but the life of absolute spirit itself, Hegel's substitute word for God—well, it is a history of all kinds of conflicts. Things don't add up. There are existential problems, that is, things that aren't rationally discordant, but nonetheless, don't work out in terms of our individual lives, and there are socioeconomic forces at work that also are part of this conflict. And they too, these socioeconomic forces at work, these kind of conflicts, are also part of the history of spirit, also part of the unfolding of the life of the divine mind. They too are part and parcel of our consciousness and the consciousness of the absolute.

Hegel has a view that's much spoofed, parodied, but we need better to understand what it is because it has even been written in a different way in the last 20 years. That view is that history has come to an end. Oh, bosh! Here you are. Here I am. It looks like history is going on. Some good things are happening. Some terrible things are happening. What Hegel meant to say by "history had come to an end" is that the life of spirit had played itself out in terms of the possibilities available to spirit. Things would keep happening, but nothing new could happen. It would just be a variation of what had already happened.

Hegel has the notion—in German, the word is *Aufhebung*, very, very hard to translate—Hegel thinks that the conflicts of history in which you and I find ourselves and history itself, understood as the unfolding of a divine consciousness, the conflicts involved, we live through and get to the other side of. We don't resolve a conflict by abandoning a conflicting element; we absorb it. That is his bold, courageous, dynamic, spirited, energetic notion of what the best could be for us in the journey of life and what the best is of the human spirit and what the meaning of life is. For Hegel, the meaning of life is to realize that we are a process, we participate in history, history has come to an end and that all history's great possibilities have played themselves out.

From Hegel's standpoint from the beginning of the 19th century, all we can do finally is to recapitulate what's already happened. The great things have been done. There are no new things to do, just variations of what's already happened. Hegel's account puts great emphasis on the role of what we could think of as great people, heroes of history. These are the people that on Hegel's account move history. They are the great ones, the ones that in some way matter and move one stage of history to the next.

If we can just pause for a moment at this point and think about this. If Hegel is right, there are these stages in history in which we find ourselves and occasionally the conflicts underlying whatever our stage in history is, becomes so powerful that there needs to be a great person, some form of hero that will emerge, who will, with courage, embrace the conflicts and find a way to the other side of the conflicts. Not so much just solve the conflicts, but live through them, absorb them and move beyond.

Hegel says—and we will see him attacked for this—that ideas are the prime movers of history—not social or economic forces, but ideas, and we are going to see this attack as our journey continues. Hegel will tell us that the meaning of history is found in ideas, that ideas move history and that what you and I can do is participate in, come to understand what these ideas have been, live with them, experience them and have fully absorbed them, and in that way, to have a full life. It is through great people that these ideas emerge. Actually, it is Hegel's view that even the people who move history, the ones who carry forward great ideas that embrace and get beyond conflicts, may not know that this is what they are doing.

Hegel calls this the *Cunning of Reason*—that somehow there is a movement that occurs and that even the great ones who forward it do not know that they are doing this. Hegel also has the notion of a great political leader. A great political leader is one who forms a context in which ideas can be pursued and culture can be developed. Hegel not only thinks ideas move history, but that there must be a context in which ideas are forwarded and it is political leaders who, in special circumstances, move us forward by creating a stable context. Hegel also tells us that what rights we possess, you and I in our journey of life, we possess within a stable context that the great leaders provide and that therefore our duties are to the context that has been provided, that allows us to move forward.

Hegel, in fact, thinking that you need a stable context that great political leaders provide, has a very activist notion of the state. The state is not just an umpire that allows people to do what they want and keeps them from colliding too often. For Hegel, a state provides cultural benefit. Further, Hegel has a notion of the philosopher. Well, the philosopher is someone who is able to understand and articulate what the great human possibilities have been. The philosopher is the person who is able to understand and be one with the highest of human possibilities. Even if these ideas are part of the past, we can recreate them in our minds and imaginations and the journey of life is to know what these great ideas were and to be able to embody them.

In this, Hegel is very influenced by a philosopher, artist, writer and politician named Johann von Goethe. Goethe lived mostly in the 18th century, but in the early 19th century said, "You must have full experience. You must experience every phase of life. Only the great ones move history forward, but each of us can re-experience and recapitulate what these phases were, what they were like and what they've contributed to the human spirit." That's an alternative vision to the spectatorial standpoint of the Greeks, where we are simply meant to know. And it is kind of a different view than an ecstatic view that comes from some religions, which mystically takes us out of experience. Hegel's idea is to recapitulate, re-experience what the dynamic ideas have been.

There is a tension in Hegel, an important tension, and we need to say something about that. Hegel thinks that there is formal morality—that is Kant's duty—but there are also concretely embedded customs. Hegel thinks Kant's formal morality—duty, duty, duty, keeps desire under tow—is too formal, too abstract. It doesn't really tell us much to do, and he thinks that human history develops in terms of customs that are embedded in communities and that we find what we will call our moral life within these communities. But of course, that raises serious problems sometimes for community members. What happens if some people, to be creative, must be in a customary or in almost any sense, immoral? What does that say about life and its meaning? What does it say about life and its meaning if you live in a community where you will go along with its customs or even a formal morality, but perhaps at the cost of creating activity? Or what is it as if creative activity requires that you break formal rules of morality or that you violate customs?

There are examples of this. Beethoven is one, perhaps. Picasso is accused of not being such a nice person, but of being very creative. Some have even said that perhaps the creativity only came because of the kind of life—not one to be thoroughly proud of—that Picasso lived. Same sort of thing has been said about James Joyce. So Hegel says we live in communities. We are embodiments of the development of the spirit, but there are conflicts that arise as a result of these circumstances. Spirit is meant to be creative, but creativity may come only through situation where we have to violate customary and formal moral standards.

What to do about this? It's been said that the great person is seldom good. It is the great person that moves history. But is it true to move history, whether to create a state, a government or a stable context? Is it true that to do that, you can't always do it as a good person? Hegel has trouble working out how it is that greatness and the kind of creativity that moves history can be reconciled with our normal moralities. He also thinks that we are caught up in situations that involved dominance and subordination. On Hegel's view, equality is hard achieved at the deepest level.

Hegel also emphasizes passion. Whereas Kant called passion a cancer, Hegel says that only is it possible for great things to emerge, only ever will they emerge as the result of great passion, the great embrace of ideas. Hegel also tells us that part of the journey of life involves that we recognize each other and that recognition of person to person in a stable context is absolutely fundamental for our enrichment.

This is heavy stuff. We've got the notion of history as God's autobiography. We see that history moves in terms of ideas. There are creative spirits who supposedly move history not always knowing that they are doing it. We have this frightful notion that maybe the great movements of history are at the cost of ordinary morals—customary, normal moral life—formal moral principles. What to say about this?

Hegel wants to write a history of human life, which says we all, in differing ways—some of us a little more knowingly, most of us not knowingly at all—have participated in a great narrative, which is the unfolding of what then we would call God's consciousness. Hegel actually does not say, though he is often accused of this, "Well, everything has worked out wonderfully, so we have all kinds of atrocities, we have all kinds of natural disasters, but history is God's story and it's a wonderful story because God is God." All Hegel finally really says about this is that you can tell a story. You can tell a story about how human history has unfolded, but make sense. It doesn't completely end the troubles; it doesn't make everything right, but there is a way of telling the story of human history through which we can say, "Yes, it actually is worth it." The human race has been something and meant something.

Maybe the journey of life, to find the meaning of life, is to be able to look back at history and say, in the midst of all the terrible things that happened, wonderful things have happened too. We can see what those wonderful things are and at least in our imagination and our thoughts, we can re-experience them. We can't go back to the Middle Ages, but we may know what it would have been like to have been medieval and absorb that too, and come to see that there is a whole world of different experiences, and maybe they come in a sequence. Even if they are played out, even if history is over, that there couldn't be anything new, maybe we can relive imaginatively what these stages have been and we can say, in effect, "Been there, done that." We can know what it has been to be human and what life is about.

This is quite a daring notion. It is a daring notion to view history as that important, a daring notion to think that the journey of life doesn't have to do altogether with your individual life, or my individual life, it has a lot more to do with the development of history and our ability imaginatively, to relive history's moments. Our ability to detect great people and see how they've embraced the most difficult of situations and gotten to the other side and maybe when they got to the other side, it has become a different world and maybe we can relive, if only in our imagination, those stages. That is Hegel's grand picture. It is a grand picture of how history can be recapitulated in us, and how we can see that great ideas, even ideas not understood at the time by the people that moved them forward, have been the elements, exactly those ideas that have moved history.

But then, what does this tell us about our freedom, your freedom and my freedom? If we are thinking about a journey toward the meaning of life and life is to be understood as a journey, where does freedom fit into Hegel's account? Are we caught in a situation where we just observe a great history that has happened? Where is our freedom in this? I've mentioned the state, the government. A stable context is necessary for us to understand these things. What role closer looked at does government and the state play in Hegel's account?

Lecture Six
Hegel on State and Society

Scope:

Hegel understands human history to be the progressive, though problematic, journey to human freedom. His notion of freedom and of human rights in general is different from and more inclusive than our Anglo-American versions. For us, rights are primarily immunities that secure us from interference. Freedom is construed as the right to be left alone to do as one wishes. Hegel understands our freedom as involving the supplementary opportunity to find our rightful needs recognized and met through those institutions and social arrangements that constitute our social and political life and are protected through our citizenship. Rights are constituted by that nexus of objective conditions that promotes free expression and the responsive acknowledgement of legitimate human needs. Hegel also provides a provocative account of the creation of states and our relation to them. He finds meaningful life in society and citizenship.

Outline

I. Hegel's account of human life in its inner nature and historical unfolding is not only understood as Absolute Spirit coming to full and articulate awareness of itself *as* Spirit. It is also construed as the difficult journey to complete human freedom.

   A. There is a problematic notion of historical and personal transition in Hegel. It is construed as a perilous challenge and as an *Übergang* (a perilous transition).

   1. Hegel believes that, living with full passion, we must commit to facing life's difficulties and getting through and beyond them.

   2. Hegel celebrates the notion of retrospective necessity. After the fact of a major decision, we can tell a story that makes that decision appear to be inevitable and sensible.

   3. Hegel has a selective theodicy involving the notion of sacrifice and elements that are irredeemably negative.

   B. Hegel understands death as a metaphor for spiritual transition.

1. Hegel does not ask if there is a life after death; he asks if there is a life after birth. He believes that we may be "deadened" by various situations and conditions in our lives.

2. Hegel construes a series of such deaths as necessary for the fruition of Spirit.

3. Hegel hopes we will live in a wholehearted, passionate way.

C. Hegel speaks not only about the whole of history but also of our individual histories.

1. We can live a history that allows us to see the past and experience what it meant.

2. We can also have a history of living forward in the future and being open to it and its conflicts.

II. Hegel's account of freedom is closely tied to his understanding of the French Revolution. This revolution itself is discussed under the heading of "Freedom and Terror" in Hegel's *Phenomenology of Spirit*.

A. Unusual circumstances surrounded the writing of the *Phenomenology of Spirit*.

1. Napoleon was seen as the *Zeitgeist* (the spirit of the time), riding one day on horseback through Jena, Germany, where Hegel used to work.

2. Hegel's own personal situation is illustrative of his conception of the meaning of history.

   a. He had a publishing deadline to meet.

   b. A young girl was expecting his child.

B. Hegel's diagnosis of the meaning of the French Revolution is provocative and controversial.

1. Institutions were needed, both political and social, that would acknowledge the needs of human beings and speak to those needs.

2. These needs must carefully be distinguished from wants.

3. It is important that individuals be able to recognize themselves in those institutions that support them and to know that they and their needs are recognized by those institutions.

> **4.** The underlying cause of revolutionary activity is the failure of these conditions to be met.

III. Hegel's understanding of human freedom is intimately related to the notions of liberties and rights.

> **A.** The Anglo-Saxon notion of right is viewed as both important and insufficient.
>
> > **1.** Rights are construed both as liberties and as immunities.
> >
> > **2.** Hegel understands this Anglo-Saxon notion as an account of subjective right, the right to be free from interference.
> >
> > **3.** Hegel believes in an essential human nature and is concerned about its notions regarding its erosion through the seduction of diffuse desires and wants.
>
> **B.** In its full, positive sense, freedom must include the recognition of one's rightful place in an order that rationally acknowledges one.

IV. Hegel accounts for the genesis of states and emphasizes their importance in the life of the human spirit.

> **A.** The Social Contract theory is insufficient as an account of society, according to Hegel.
>
> > **1.** There is no general will that is operative prior to the formation of the state.
> >
> > **2.** Contractarian theory fails, for transactions cannot be legitimated outside of a preexisting legal nexus.
>
> **B.** Hegel claims that states are formed through the compelling acts of illustrious individuals.
>
> > **1.** States are the result of coercive activities.
> >
> > **2.** Once formed, states have an objective status and duties to them precede rights within them.
> >
> > **3.** Freedom and rights are the freedom and rights of humans, and humans can only exist within those structures constituted by the states.
>
> **C.** At a later stage in his career, Hegel celebrates the middle class and commercial society because of three of its features.
>
> > **1.** It has the rule of rationally based law.

2. In it, objective rights are in place and are acknowledged. Action must be in accordance with them.

3. The right to private property is recognized. It is involved in self-recognition. For Hegel, it is required if one is to be fully recognized as a person.

V. Important differences exist between the younger and the more established Hegel.

   A. The younger Hegel is favorable to revolution.

      1. The emphasis is on process.

      2. Political tendencies are toward the Left.

      3. Hegel looks to the transcendence of institutional religion.

   B. The established Hegel is far more conservative in disposition.

      1. The emphasis is on the system.

      2. Political tendencies are to the right of center.

      3. Hegel wishes to conserve gains and is celebratory.

Essential Reading:

Georg Wilhelm Friedrich Hegel, *Elements of the Philosophy of Right*.

Herbert Marcuse, *Reason and Revolution: Hegel and the Rise of Social Theory*.

Supplementary Reading:

Karl Löwith, *From Hegel to Nietzsche: The Revolution in Nineteenth-Century Thought*.

Questions to Consider:

1. What does Hegel mean by freedom, and how does it differ from our ordinary conception of freedom?

2. If Hegel is correct, what is our relation to the state?

Lecture Six—Transcript
Hegel on State and Society

In our last lecture together, we looked at Hegel's extraordinary conception of history. And in terms of that conception, there is really a narrative. Hegel thinks he has given a rational account of history. It is not Kant's austere account, but it is a notion of history as having a story to it, and we can come to know what that story is. Hegel also says nothing great happens without passion. That is to say, it is also passion and the embrace of conflict and struggle that has moved history along.

Unlike the Romantics, who were less concerned about history and more concerned about the idiosyncratic, Hegel has taken the creative and the passionate and fused them with the rational, and out of that, we really have a story to tell. And it is in fact, God's autobiography, the coming to full consciousness of the divine life. And maybe that life has been complete and nothing can be added to it, but Hegel thinks that it can be recapitulated. Well, that is not going to be possible for everybody.

There may have been creative spirits who did it. There may be great statespeople who created stable contexts in which that kind of life could be lived. But what about—what I will call hesitantly—normal people, such as perhaps you and me—certainly me—we are not the creative ones. We are not necessarily altogether fully going to be able to understand all its ins and outs. What is our life then going to be like? And what Hegel tells us is that we need to reflect on the way government is, the way states are, and the extent to which freedom can be found within the context of life lived today in a state.

Hegel's account of human life and the inner nature of human life isn't just understood as what he's called "absolute spirit," coming to full and articulate awareness of itself; he also understands history as the development and the difficult journey to complete human freedom, not just a grand story of the unfolding of the life of the divine, but it can also be even in our time, the notion that we too can become, in our time, fully free.

But what does that mean? Let's consider, there is a problematic notion in Hegel. It involves a personal transition, an historical one that bears close attention. It involves a perilous challenge. It involves a transition. The German word for it is *Übergang*, and that has to be understood as a very perilous transition, that if Hegel is right, is part of the meaning of life—part of the meaning of life, the journey toward the meaning of life involves embracing, looking right in the face of extraordinary difficulties, fundamental conflicts, conflict that we must somehow find a way to get beyond. And Hegel thinks if we live with full passion and we are committed to embracing the conflicts that we face, we will find a way to move beyond them—not avoid them—but move beyond them. We can never predict in advance how this will be done. But it can be done and it would involve in a certain way, a kind of courageous leap, not knowing for sure what will be on the other side.

What Hegel does tell us is that on the journey of life, having gone through such a transition, we can in fact look back retrospectively and we can see that there is a story that can be told about the transition that we make. Hegel is very strange in this way. Hegel has the notion that as we live life forward, we cannot know in advance as we embrace wholeheartedly conflict and contradiction. We cannot know in advance how we can move through to the other side of it. And that will involve an element of uncertainty. This is one of the great fascinating, dangerous notions in Hegel. But Hegel also claims that on the other side, we can look back and there will always be a story we can tell in retrospect that will say what we did made sense. It is part of a thread of development. We couldn't have anticipated it in advance that we would land where we landed, but in retrospect, it makes great sense.

Is the journey of life the embracing of such conflicts, and having to undergo such transitions? And is it a story that is always a good story? Hegel says there will always be irredeemably negative elements in any story we tell that is the story of our lives, but these negative elements we have to absorb, because our life is not just everything that happens. Our life, and the meaning of our life, is the story that we can tell about it as a narrative—as a narrative that allows us to say, "Here is how it has happened, and there is a way to explain my journey that makes sense of it." The journey I have made may have involved agonies, difficulties, sacrifices, but it was not for nothing. There is a story that can be told about it. And to live a life that allows a story of this sort to be told about it—that is what the journey of life is about. In important ways, that's what the meaning of life is.

Hegel has some unusual, perhaps even extraordinary, things to say about death. He understands death as a metaphor for spiritual transition. You could say, as many have said, that the problem isn't—and it wasn't for Hegel—whether there is a life after death, the question is, is there a life after birth? Is it possible that we can be dead within this life? And if we are dead within this life, how does this happen? What does it mean? What Hegel tells us is that we can be deadened—deadened within situations that perhaps we don't understand and we step back and experience confusion that we don't try to resolve. Hegel also says that we can be deadened by being caught up in sociopolitical circumstances—that perhaps even if we understand them, we feel stalemated and locked in by them. Or we can be dead in a way that isn't just simply a matter of understanding, not simply a matter of sociopolitical circumstances that imprison us—we could also be locked in, in such a way that we could say it's a kind of existential agony.

Hegel says that if we can see experience, allow ourselves to understand that we may have been deadened, then maybe we can open ourselves; we can embrace the circumstance or situation into which we have found ourselves deadened. And by bringing that situation to life, and courageously and wholeheartedly living with it, we will bring ourselves to life. This is a dynamic notion of Hegel, the notion that many lives—many, many lives—are lived in a deadened and anesthetized way; many lives are locked in by conventions, but also by conflicts that are deepened not understood. Therefore, we lead a kind of death in life, and what Hegel wants us to do is open ourselves, live in a wholehearted way that will embrace what they otherwise have stymied and stifled us and opened us up to our future. This is at the heart of the work of the early Hegel.

What we have to understand is that Hegel not only talks about the whole of history as the history of the human spirit understood as the unfolding of the divine life—Hegel is also prepared and talks about the journey of life as our individual histories. And those histories can be lived in at least two ways. We can live a history that allows us to see the past and experience imaginatively what it meant, but there could also be the history of living forward into the future, not avoiding conflict, but being open to it and open to it in a way that allows us to absorb it and transcend it.

Let's keep track, as we go forward, that after Hegel, a lot of people are going to say, "But that's just a dream; how few people could do that." Hegel is just talking to the extraordinary individual. Could we possibly understand the journey of life toward meaning, to be looking at our lives as if—and perhaps it would be true—we are caught up in deadened situations; that underlying them, there are conflicts, and that we have somehow to open up ourselves to these situations, that we have to try to go beyond them? Doesn't that sound all too grand? Hegel seems to have two problems then for us. Hegel has a notion of history as the big story. But here we are, and Hegel has a notion of passionate, courageous individuals—passionate, creative individuals, courageous, who just embrace life, live it to the full, take on, come to understand conflict and creatively go beyond it. But is this possible?

If it is possible, we would at least have to be free. And Hegel's notion of what it is to be free is very close to his understanding of the French Revolution. He discusses the French Revolution in his early work, in a work called *The Phenomenology of Spirit*, which was published in 1807. And he discusses the French Revolution in a part of this work, called "Freedom and Terror." He thinks that freedom and terror tells us a lot about the French Revolution. He also thinks freedom and terror properly understood—well, they tell us a lot about our individual lives.

Unusual circumstances surrounded Hegel's writing of the *Phenomenology of Spirit* and the section on freedom and terror. At this time, Napoleon was coming through the city where Hegel was writing his book. And Hegel looked out his window, saw Napoleon and said to a friend, "We've just seen the world spirit riding through on horseback." Odd. But you see, this was Hegel's sense of things, that there are people that move history, that they could also be ordinary people as you just looked at them: "There is a man on a horse." But at the same time, Hegel thought, "That man on the horse, warts and all, is one of those who is moving history." And Hegel's own situation was equally problematic (not that Napoleon's was that problematic). But Hegel's situation was that he had a publisher's deadline to meet—how to put this delicately—a young woman was pregnant and Hegel would be the father, and he was pressured by the publisher and the fighting was going on, and what to do? And Hegel said, "Well, that's sort of the way history is. You're caught up in immediate particular circumstances that could overwhelm you, and at the same time, you have a purpose in something that you are meant to do." And these things get scrambled together and the important thing in human life is to know what does matter and what doesn't matter.

And this actually would take us back to something we talked about before. Maybe that Hegel would be a father; maybe that there is a publisher's deadline; maybe these things mattered too. But on Hegel's account, what really mattered was the development of spirit, the life of ideas, so that finally what mattered was the book—the book was what really mattered.

Now, with regard to the French Revolution, which Hegel wrote about in the section called "Freedom and Terror," Hegel says that institutions are important, very important. We need political and social institutions. But we need them in a particular way. Political and social institutions must be of such a sort that they acknowledge our needs as human beings, they speak to those needs, and we feel thereby acknowledged and recognized. We must be surrounded by institutions that recognize us as human being.

Quickly, Hegel tells us, that isn't really the full story. Just think of all the wants we have as opposed to the needs we have. Institutions don't have simply to be set up to take care, to cater to our various wants. They must distinguish between wants and needs, and speak to needs, not just to wants. And that is the importance of institutions. And we must feel that our true rational needs are recognized, acknowledged and spoken to by institutions. Hegel's claim was that the underlying cause of revolutionary activity was that these conditions weren't met and that that's why the French Revolution occurred in the way it did. If we can just pause for a moment, I'd like you to consider something as we move along in our journey.

There is an old metaphysical principle in philosophy. It is that something is better than nothing. Hegel suggests to us that sometimes nothing is better than something, that you could be in a situation where your needs are not acknowledged or recognized, the institutions around you are not speaking to you and therefore, you are in a situation of virtually complete abandonment and alienation. And if in that sense, you are not recognized, if in that sense you have nothing, perhaps there is nothing to lose in the radical attempt to change things altogether.

Hegel's own notion of freedom is intimately related to notions of liberties and rights. Hegel's view, a European view, is different than the Anglo-Saxon notions that we typically have of rights and liberties. Hegel thinks that those Anglo-Saxon notion are insufficient. They are important, but they don't tell the full story. If we were to believe Hegel, how the Anglo-Saxon world understands rights, are in part as immunities, you have the right not to be interfered with. You have the liberty to be left alone.

And Hegel calls that subjective right. He even applauds it in people who have a kind of conscience that's left alone to speak its mind and is not interfered with. But he says, "You are not fully free if you are just left alone to say what you want." If you just have the subjective right not to be interfered with, of course it is important to do as you wish. But if there is no supportive context in which you do what you do, then that's not complete freedom. The freedom that you have by being left alone is part of the story, but it needs to be supplemented by something. And what Hegel supplements it by is the notion of an essential human nature that we have. And he thinks that it can be eroded, this essential human nature we have, by various diffused desires and wants that we might have—we may be lowered by that. Hegel thinks that we have to not just give in to wants and desires; we can't just be left alone, but Hegel also thinks that the objective circumstances—the institutional social circumstances—in which we find ourselves, must speak to us, and speak to us in such a way that we experience that we count, that we are acknowledged, that our so-called rational life is understood. And by "rational life," Hegel by no means means our reason alone, but our essential life as human beings, with cultural hopes, with religious feelings, with a sense that we need participation and a social and political order that is a little greater than we have when we are just left alone to do what we want.

Let's consider further—in maybe a full positive sense, freedom has got to involve the recognition of our rightful place in an order that does truly and fully acknowledge us. But how do we get such an order? How does that happen? Hegel has an unusual account of how governments and states are generated, and he emphasizes how important they are in human life. Hegel says, for example, that you can't be fully human without a stable, governmental, social context, and that it is very important to understand how such a context comes about. He says that something that is called the "social contract theory" doesn't explain how a state comes about; it is insufficient. You would have to have already a stable context for people then to sit down and work out rules about how they are going to get along with each other, but how does the stable context first emerge? You just don't have a situation where people sit down and work things out because already there must be stability presupposed to do that.

Well then, Hegel thinks, what about a Contractarian theory? Maybe there can be contracts among groups of people. But he says, "No, that isn't the way states could come about either. They couldn't come about that way because there has to be some preexisting legal nexus. You couldn't use contracts or the social contract theory." Well, we now have a problem. Hegel says that you need the context of a state to flourish, but he doesn't quite yet explain how it comes to flourish. And the answer he gives should worry us. It should worry us as individuals that live our lives in the world, who see life as a journey and wonder if life has a meaning, because Hegel says that states are the result of coercive activities. He thinks that particular individuals have illustrious powers, magnetic, almost charismatic powers that create a stable context of which life can be lived. And because you need the state in which to live life, your duties to the state that allows you to live a full life are more important than your rights within that state. And that, to some, of course, is somewhat a frightening notion.

Hegel says that the very notion of freedom, the very notion of rights or the freedom, the rights of human beings, can only exist within the context of a state. This is a problem. This is something that we need to think carefully about. Is this true? Is it true that a stable context is needed? Is it true that our duties within such a stable context are deeper and more important than any rights we might have? Hegel sounds like someone who some call a statist, who puts the state ahead of the individual. His way of explaining this would be to say full freedom isn't just being left alone, it is having a context in which to flourish, but you pay a real price for that.

Generally, Hegel has—and this is a Hegel who is 20 and 25 years into his successful career. This is a Hegel that now doesn't talk so much about the life of the spirit, doesn't talk so much about the unfolding of the divine consciousness, doesn't talk so much about the struggles, the conflicts, the bringing of a dead life to full life. Hegel, at this later stage in his career, thinks—or at least this is what he is accused of—that maybe the journey of life at a certain point is complete. We have found ourselves in a stable context, maybe even—and this is what Hegel's successors say and they sneer at him about it—maybe it is a life of that strange thing called a professor in a Middle Class society, a commercial society where you can buy and sell. And it is a society that has rationally-based laws, and objective rights are in place and are acknowledged. And we all see that our actions can, should and will be, in accordance with it.

Hegel even goes further in this direction. He says you must have private property. That is because you can't be a full person without private property, and you couldn't be fully recognized unless you could recognize yourself as having it and others recognize you as having it. This begins to look like what? Hegel's accusers say he has sold out. Hegel—the great adventurer of the spirit, who had claimed to know the journey of life as knowing the great ideas and reliving them in the mind, Hegel, who thought of struggle—now seems to be a Hegel that says, "We've got to have the state. We have duties to it. And it must have a certain structure that though it supports us, underlying at all, that is where our duties are."

Has Hegel sold out? Or has Hegel just realized that when we are young, we adventure. We take risks. We take on things that are unusual and looking back at them, maybe they even frighten us that we did them. But then we have the older Hegel, who says, "Now we've got the journey somewhat completed, and here we are living the full life." And the full life for Hegel is one in a full society. So the young Hegel, if not radical-adventuresome—caught up in process, life—is a courageous adventurer. And the political tendencies some thought of that young Hegel or to the left. And he wanted to transcend all kinds of things, including institutional religion.

But now, the established Hegel, 20 years later, having left behind this grand vision of a dynamic life, becomes very conservative in this position. The emphasis is on the system. The political tendencies tend to go right of center, and Hegel wants to conserve gains and celebrate what is.

We are going to be looking, as we move forward, at a distinction between ideas that come out of the early Hegel—ideas of a dynamic process of development, a celebration of, for instance, the French Revolution as overturning certain institutions to liberate the human spirit. And then we are going to be looking at reactions based on celebrations of that early Hegel. We are going to be looking at reactions to that by people who look at this Hegel who comes up 20 years later. Maybe by then he is a full professor. Time for change is over. What we've got to do is get these young Turks in place, where everything has got to fall inline as with the establishment. And Hegel tells all of us, perhaps it is with great celebration, that he, the professor in Prussia and Berlin, has looked around Prussian society and it has actually captured the way things ought to be.

Some people will view the young Hegel as adolescent; others as having a vision that, when he got older, he sold out. And some will view the older Hegel as sober and realistic. After all, when you are young, life is a journey; you can look for its meaning. When you get tenure and a full professorship, those problems are over and you look to the establishment to conserve and preserve things for you.

But look now where we stand. Look at the route we've taken so far, because we are about to make still another transition. We've looked at the rational Kant. We can't know how things are, we must use our reason, but we can't know how things are and will live morally in terms of reason. We've looked at the Romantics. We must look beyond the rational to the nonrational. And we have looked at Hegel, who says, on the one hand, history has been a great adventure. We can understand it. In some ways we live it, if only in our minds and imaginations, and we've looked now just very recently at a Hegel who says, "If the institutions around you support you in a certain way, you've arrived."

But in all of our talks, we have not concentrated quite yet on the notion of the Self. Who is the Self that might use reason, this Self that might become romantic and use creativity, this Self in history? Who is this Self that struggles, who looks for the meaning of life, who is on the journey? It is the notion of Self that we will look at next.

Lecture Seven
Hegel on Selfhood and Human Identity

Scope:

What emerges in and through Hegel is a conception of *Self* involving relational elements—as if the *Self* were as much a *relating* as a "thing" standing in *relation*. At first, this conception may seem counterintuitive. There have been a number of quite natural reasons for understanding the *Self* on an underlying level as singular and as a unity. After reviewing the various political, religious, and everyday grounds for this "billiard ball" view, consideration is given to the relational alternative that derives from Hegel. Much philosophical guidance for living draws from it, even while partially rejecting it. On this account, there are (at least) three dimensions to our selfhood. Included is our own conception of ourselves. But also the manner in which "others" might be said to contribute to our constitution as *Selves*. Primary consideration is given to the nature and changeability of our self-conception over time, and how others are decisive in such matters.

Outline

I. The "billiard ball" conception of what a person *is*—an item distinguishable from its relation to other items—has been very influential in Western thinking. However, it has seldom been dwelled upon as a concept. In some ways, it is so commonsensical that it could hardly draw a great deal of attention.

   A. Even so, the "billiard ball" conception is not easy to think beyond and thus to escape.

      1. In the "billiard ball" conception, each of us is a quite separate and distinct individuality, a single something, a simple, underlying unit.

      2. This conception arises in part from the longstanding, obvious commonsense experience that each of us inhabits a separate, physical body and thus reality.

3. It is our further experience that we know the contents of our own minds directly, but we have only inferential knowledge—or need to accept on faith—what is occurring in the minds of others. We are "we." They are "they."

4. The "billiard ball" conception is given further impetus by religious doctrines that construe souls as distinct from bodies and make each individual responsible for his or her own soul, itself an interiority out of the reach of others.

B. Still further impetus for the "billiard ball" theory is lent by moral and legal doctrines that stress individual responsibility and culpability.

1. Political developments increasingly stress the rights of individuals not to be interfered with *as* individuals.

2. Political and economic developments in an increasingly capitalistic, entrepreneurial world stress private property, the significance of individual initiative, and opportunities for individual achievement.

II. In Hegel, we find an alternative to what I am calling the "billiard ball" doctrine. This alternative is very influential, for, even when modified or rejected, it retains extraordinary force in the history of ideas.

A. A person might be said to have three dimensions, each constitutive of person—or selfhood. Our concern in this lecture is primarily with two of these dimensions.

1. People have conceptions of themselves. We do not live without them.

2. The conception that a person has of himself or herself is not extraneous, like clothing. It is a part of the person or, alternatively, the person is embedded in the conception constitutively. This conception is the *first dimension* of personhood.

3. Paradoxically, even if a self-conception is not in accord with the Self it conceives, it is nonetheless part of that person and has no mere secondary status. This is the *second dimension* of personhood: self images or conceptions, whether accurate or not.

4. Even if that conception changed to a different, equally "inaccurate" conception, it would mean that, to a considerable extent, the person would have become a different sort of person.

B. Three somewhat extreme cases are worth mentioning.

1. A person may be *so* out of touch that we call that person psychotic.

2. A person may have virtually no horizon, no perspective regarding himself or herself, that is, a person so completely "one with self" that he or she has no imagination, no scope, no tension.

3. Self-deception is the most intriguing case: Is the "cure" for self-deception a coming to terms with one's *real* person? Or is the *real* person the one that is being cured?

    a. Some have said that self-deception is an essential part of our creative nature.

    b. In peeling away conceptions of self, where does one arrive? This process poses a conundrum.

III. Whatever humans turn out to be, a relationship is involved.

A. The two *relata* are the Self and that Self's image (understanding, conception) with respect to itself.

B. A further element, a *third dimension*, comes into focus when we consider the nature and sources of conceptions of ourselves.

1. Often—in fact, invariably—various institutions and historical circumstances in which we grow up contribute to our conception of ourselves.

2. These circumstances are not of our own making. Coming about through *others*, they nonetheless are involved in our self-understanding.

3. Others thus enter into the constitution of who we are. Had they made—or were they to make—our social, historical, and/or institutional circumstances different, we would understand ourselves differently. We would be different persons than we are, quite probably even different *kinds* of persons.

4. Essential to historicism is the claim that our natures change over time because of changes in historical circumstances. As for the "billiard ball" model, historicism is either false or makes no sense at all.

5. Central to these conflicting views is the distinction between internal and external relations.

IV. Based on what might be called the historicist model, it is possible to talk altogether coherently about "losing one's identity."

A. Again, part of who a person is—one's identity—is one's understanding of oneself, and that understanding involves constitutive and nutritional elements provided by one's (historical) circumstances.

B. The loss of, or an abrupt change in, these circumstances will alter and initially cause people to lose their sense of who they are.

1. If they have or are identified with such circumstances, the alteration of these circumstances will bring about at least a partial loss of their sense of identity.

2. The language of religion can give us an example of this experience. St. Augustine writes engagingly regarding the notion of *losing* oneself in order to *find* oneself.

Essential Reading:

Isaiah Berlin, *Four Essays on Liberty*.

Charles Taylor, *Sources of the Self: The Making of the Modern Identity*.

Supplementary Reading:

Karl Löwith, *From Hegel to Nietzsche: The Revolution in Nineteenth-Century Thought*.

Questions to Consider:

1. What sense does it make to claim that there are differing dimensions to our Selfhood?

2. Do the conceptions that we have of ourselves make a difference as to who we actually are?

Lecture Seven—Transcript
Hegel on Selfhood and Human Identity

Let's take a moment to consider where we are now on our journey together. In our last time together, we talked about the role of the state. If you'll remember, the claim was made that you do need a state as a stable context. But there was also a worry that perhaps a state, in order to give security, may also take away certain things that might be important to us. It is very much true that the critics of Hegel worried about that development in Hegel. We've also looked now— and I don't quite think we've looked enough—at the notion of freedom. On the one hand, freedom could mean "to be left alone." On the other hand, true freedom might mean that we're in a context that supports and acknowledges us. After all, you cannot be fully free if you're in a totally, totally alienated environment.

But in all of this sort-of-reflection and conversation that we're having, we haven't given close consideration to the notion of the Self. Who would it be? Who are we that live in the state? Or, maybe are in some sense, outsiders. Who are we that are the kinds of people who concern ourselves with the creative life and perhaps reflecting on what history means and where it's brought us? But there's a certain conception of the Self, of the person, that I'm going to call the "billiard ball" conception of what a person is. This conception, the "billiard ball" conception, takes ourselves as distinguishable from all other selves, as separate items. You are you. I am I. Each person is the person that that person is. That's been a very, very influential view in the course of Western thinking.

What it suggests is that the journey of life, whatever it is, is a journey that perhaps each of us may quite separately experience, and there is a very distinct difference, call it an absolute difference, between individuals. Now this perhaps hasn't been dwelled on as much as it should be dwelled on, and that's because in some ways, it's commonsensical. Your life is yours; mine is mine. We each go our ways. We may cross paths. We may do some things together, but basically each of us is a separate individual. So this "billiard ball" notion, as I've called it, is so commonsensical that it perhaps has not been given the consideration it deserves. In many ways, it's hard to think beyond, it's hard to escape, and yet let's look at it more closely. Let's look at this notion that each of us is a single something—that each of us is, or has, our nature as a simple underlying unit.

How did we get this conception? What makes it as commonsensical as it does? Well, it arises from commonsense experience. Look, each of us has a separate body, a separate reality. You are somewhere, hearing, seeing—perhaps both—hearing and seeing me. I am where I am. When you see this, if you do, when you hear it, you will be somewhere, I will be somewhere else. That's so obvious. Why would we think beyond that? It's our further experience that you know the content of your mind but not the content, now, of my mind. Or the people around you, they may tell you what's on their mind but you don't necessarily know for sure that what's on their minds as they tell you is what's really on their minds. I mean, I hope what's on your mind is, "Well, this is enjoyable and intriguing and I hope I've made some sense of it as we go along," and what my mind has in it is, "I want to engage you more in these ideas." But however that goes, your mind is your mind, you are where you are; my mind is my mind, and I am where I am.

The "billiard ball" conception, as I've called it, is given even further impetus by religious doctrines. Religious doctrines that construe us, among other things, as either being or having souls that are distinct from our bodies, and the notion that each of us is responsible for our own lives, our own souls, and that if there is something like salvation, or the beyond or the meaning of life, that you're responsible for yours and I'm responsible for mine. That reinforces this "billiard ball" notion. But it's given even further impetus by various moral and legal doctrines that stress individual responsibility and culpability. We are impressed with the notion that each of us is responsible for our actions. We also have political doctrines that we talked about our last time together, and that is that we are separate individuals, not to be interfered with. Yes, we can freely join together, but we are not meant to be interfered with otherwise. We are to be left alone and respected as the individuals that we are.

Of course, in an entrepreneurial world, in a capitalist world (as we know it) that stresses private property, the significance of individual initiative, and opportunities for individual achievement and advancement, more and more we have this notion of the individual, the separate individual. An individual, who may join freely with other individuals. But your body is your body, mine is mine. Your mind is your mind, mine is mine. You will be held responsible for what you do. I will be held responsible for what I do. And if we put all those things together it seems so obvious that we are separate and distinct individuals that I suppose you'd even wonder why I've bothered to tell you this. Well, do I have something else to tell you now! I've just begun.

Now we come to the complication; we find it in an alternative doctrine provided to us by Hegel. It's very influential and even when it's modified, even when it's rejected, it has had an extraordinary force in the history of ideas. It is the notion that we are not isolated, "billiard ball" individuals, freely choosing or perhaps forced into certain relations, but nonetheless separate individuals. The doctrine that we see emerging in Hegel is that there are actually three dimensions that constitute our personhood or selfhood, and what we're really concerned with is to look at these dimensions.

Let's start with an obvious one that we've mentioned before: people have conceptions of themselves. They have images of themselves, ideas regarding themselves, and we can't live without them. We are people with ideas regarding who we are as people. What Hegel suggests is that the conceptions, the ideas we have of ourselves are not extraneous, like clothing. It isn't as if we are who we are and our conceptions of ourselves, if we're lucky, we can change like we change clothes and they're external to us. The conceptions we have of ourselves, Hegel thinks, are intimately part of us. What that means, in part, is that if we have different conceptions of ourselves, in some important ways, we would be different people than we are. Let's pause for a moment to think about this. Think of life as a journey. We are looking for the meaning of life, if there is one. Our selves are involved in this journey. But now we get the idea that maybe part of the journey of life is involved with understanding better the conception we have of ourselves, and perhaps then finding a way to alter that conception. The idea is that if you know what the conception of yourself is, if it's possible to alter it, you will become, in some way, a slightly different person. It's possible that part of the meaning of life is that alteration of our conception of our selves.

Now we need to look at something pretty paradoxical in this. What Hegel believes to be true, and many philosophers, is that even if your conception of yourself is not in accord with you, even if it's a little bit ajar in relation to you, it's also part of you. This is the notion that self-conception is more intimate than clothing, and even if your self-conception is ajar, it's equally as much part of you as the "you" in relation to which it's ajar. Think about that for just a moment. That even if your conception of yourself was askew, that too, and almost equally, is part of who you really are. Part of what you really are is not just the underlying something. Now even if that conception changed to a different equally inaccurate conception, it would mean that to a considerable extent you would still have become a different person. So alterations in self-conception, accurate or inaccurate (whatever that might mean), make us different people. That's well beyond a "billiard ball" notion of the person.

Now there are three extreme cases worth mentioning that will help us understand better what we're thinking about. You can imagine a person so out of touch, having such a strange conception of himself, or herself, that we would call that person psychotic. Now that notion, that we could be so out of touch with ourselves, that our conception of ourselves (deranged, if you want to call it), would still be part of us—that's really hard to accept. There's another kind of person— that's the kind of person who we say has virtually no horizon at all. That's the kind of person whose perception of self hugs the self so much that we say that kind of person has no imagination, has no scope, has no self-perspective, has no sense of irony. So we seem to want to play between two notions: a conception of self so out of touch that we say that, "This person is in real trouble" and a conception of self that's so close, that we say, "What a dull, unimaginative person!" A person who is so one with oneself, as we say it, no scope, no conflict, no stress, no tension, and if we're to believe people like Hegel, you need scope, stress, conflict, and tension to have that kind of dynamic self, as opposed to what I've called the "billiard ball" self that matters so much to Hegel.

There's one more case to consider in this notion that self and its conception of itself are equally important, and that's the notion of self-deception. It's a kind of the most intriguing case we could come up with. We say that many people are in self-deception. We also say that maybe people want to cure that. Some people have said that self-deception is fundamental to our nature but have also said that even though it's fundamental to our nature and makes us human, we should try to cure it. Well, there's a further reflection on this that we'll have to think about a great deal: it's the idea that perhaps self-deception is the sort of thing that if it's not too extreme, but if there's a little bit of discord between itself and its image, or idea of itself, maybe in that middle ground a dynamism exists that is the potential for our creative self.

Let's consider one other idea, and that is the idea that what we might want to do is to peel away various conceptions that we have of ourselves. We may want to accept that whether self-deception or not, it is a matter of fact the case that we have different layers in ourselves. We're not "billiard balls." Whatever we are, there are different layers of self-understanding. But if you peel things off, if you viewed even the journey of life as peeling away layers, where would you get? There's a fascinating account by the Norwegian playwright, Henrik Ibsen. In one play called *Peer Gynt*, he has the notion of the self as like an onion and you peel away, and you peel away, and you peel away, and you'd peel away, but in the end there would only be peelings; there would never be a core. Now this we need to think about. We've talked about some complex things during our time now together. On the one view, if you peeled away, you'd get a billiard ball, and you'd say, "I've finally found it!" On another view, you wouldn't ever quite get to the billiard ball, but it would be there. But the kind of tensions/conflicts/problems between the billiard ball and its various, sometimes strange ways of understanding itself—those would be the great things, the dynamic things, the creative things, that make life worth living, that give it is dynamism.

How to take this? What to say about it? Do we find anything at our core? Do we find something that's the real "us" at our core? The proverbial "billiard ball?" Or should we view human life as the journey of life—always a tension involving a core and layers that are in or out of touch with the core, but in a certain, curious way, almost better out of touch, because in being out of touch, there's creative tension. That's a romantic tension that we look at when we looked before at the Romantics; we had the notion of a life that's sought unity, fusion, but it was built out of creative conflict. We've looked at Hegel, and the notion that "Oh, you embrace conflict" and life is bringing to life, out of death, great conflicts and experiences that need to be made living. But then, how do we understand this self? Is it, when all is said and done, a billiard ball? Is it a dynamic tension? Let us consider.

Whatever we are as human beings, and I think in our journey together, what life might mean, whatever is involved, a relationship is involved. And we've come to see that two of them are related—our selves and our images, our conceptions with respect to ourselves—but there's a third dimension, a very important dimension. It comes into focus if we consider where our various conceptions of ourselves, our ideas, come from. What are their sources? What are the sources of the ways in which we experience and understand ourselves? What we see comes through very strongly in Hegel; we've thought about it, at the various institutions and historical circumstances in which we find ourselves and into which we grow up. These contribute to our conception of ourselves. So that means that we were living in the Middle Ages, which we're not. Then, the circumstances of the Middle Ages would form in some degree our conception of ourselves.

If we live in an advanced liberal democracy in the 21st century that would provide many of the elements that would feed our conception of ourselves, we mustn't have the idea that our conception of ourselves just mysteriously bubbles up from within us. If we were to believe Hegel, it's not the case that it works that way. Our conceptions—however much they are in tension with our underlying, maybe mysterious Self—those conceptions of ourselves are partly generated, partly structured, partly constituted, given their fabric by the historical circumstances in which we find ourselves living. Even though they come about through other people, they nonetheless are evolved in our understanding of ourselves, and they are also part of us. That means that, in an important way, others enter into who we are. Had they made, or were they to make our social, historical and/or institutional circumstances differently than they did, we would understand ourselves differently. We would be different people than we are, maybe even different *kinds* of people.

There's a view we haven't said much about and we need to. It's called by some, "historicism," and is the claim that our natures change over time because of changes in historical circumstances. If that is true, then the meaning of life would be a quest that would take on a different form as a journey in a different historical period. That is to say that, if we understand life as embedded in history, then the particular history of our time will determine how we can construe the journey, and how we can construe the result that the journey is supposed to lead to. Now on the "billiard ball" model, that doesn't make sense. We are who we are. History happens, but it's external to our true nature. Importantly—very, very central to these conflicting views that I'm putting before you—is a distinction between internal and external relations.

There's a famous story—so famous, it's hard to believe it's true—of a professor that once threw a piece of chalk over his back. (This was in an all-men's school many years ago.) He said, "Gentlemen, I've just changed the coast of China." What he was claiming was, what's true of the coast of China is any truth about it, and I suppose the chalk ran a few feet in one direction, so the chalk was a little closer or further from China and everyone in the class laughed, but it was that professor's way of saying that "maybe all relations are internal," whereas most of the class, the gentlemen would have said, "Oh my, when is the class over? Obviously the coast of China hasn't been changed. This is pretty nutty." But at the heart of doing something like that is the notion of what is really a relation you sustain—perhaps institutional, perhaps historical—that you think is internal to whom you are. There are certain types of relations you enter into that are intimate to you; you may not create them but they make a great difference as to how you experience yourself and how you see whom you are, whereas there are other relations that are quite external.

Let us look now, take a pause and reflect that there is a notion that we see around us very frequently. I think it's a notion that has lived historically for centuries. We see it in magazines. We see it in all kinds of places. It's the notion that one could lose one's identity. Now, what does it mean to say that one could lose one's identity? Well, if part of who you are is your understanding of yourself, and that understanding involves nutritional elements that are provided by your historical circumstances, then I'd suppose that if you were put in a quite different environment, you would have lost part of who you are. Remember, a little earlier I said there's the notion the Romantics had that basically, we are meant to be "wanderers"; that we never should never fully try to find a home in this world. There is the notion that it's important to find a home, important to find an identity, but there's also the notion that maybe it is better to have abrupt changes that allow us not to get fully invested, fully involved, in a certain way of being in a certain setting.

What about abrupt changes? If we have and undergo abrupt changes, and part of who we are is how others have formed the world in which we find ourselves fitting, is it true that there has been some form of identity loss that has occurred? Is this plausible? On the "billiard ball" model, this would make no sense at all. Even on a model that says, "I am who I am. Maybe how I understand myself is imperfect, but I'm not influenced by others, and wouldn't allow myself to be," it wouldn't make sense either. But if you think of part of your life and part of who you are—part of your selfhood—is embedded in circumstances not of your own making, but in terms of which you nonetheless live your life, then this is a very important notion: that if you are radically altered and taken from an environment that you have experienced as where you belong or think you might belong, you will experience "identity loss."

The language and experience of religion can give us examples of this. One example comes from Saint Augustine. He writes engagingly about losing oneself in order to *find* oneself. We know that that's a deep religious conception: that perhaps to find yourself, you have to lose yourself. But that might mean that what you need to do is lose one sense you have of your identity and come through being in a different kind of circumstance to reach a different sense of identity. That would involve at least two things: an alteration of your deep connection with the world, and possibly as a result of that alteration in your deep conception of your situation, a fundamental change in you. These are complicated ideas, complicated to capture and to sort out, and what we will see soon is that numerous philosophers take parts of what we have been talking about today and reject them. Other philosophers take the parts that the previous philosophers rejected and say, "These are the ones that matter." We are going to see some philosophers emphasize that how we experience ourselves is fundamental, and we are going to see other philosophers say that the historical circumstances, the political institutional circumstances in find ourselves embedded, *these* are what matter.

So far, it's not been all bad if we measure this on an optimistic/pessimistic scale. After all, Hegel was an optimist. Kant, actually, was an optimist. The Romantics thought it would be struggle, but one could be an optimist about the future of the human spirit. But optimism isn't the only story we can tell. We are going to turn now as our next adventure, in our next journey together, to a very, very pessimistic point of view. This is the point of view of a philosopher named Arthur Schopenhauer. We'll have to be steeled and ready for this because Schopenhauer will give us many reasons to think life as we know it is really awful.

Lecture Eight
Schopenhauer's Pessimism

Scope:

Is there truly a human predicament—and might there be some direct access to ourselves—that better reveals to us our composition and thus those components that we must come to terms with in any guiding of our lives? An unusual presence in philosophy, Arthur Schopenhauer (1788–1860) offers an account of our nature that is most bleak, earning him the title of pessimist. His own life makes his pessimism more likely. This life is explored in the light of the soon-spreading notion that philosophies are confessions of temperament, not objective insights into valid life strategies. Regarding external reality, Schopenhauer aligns himself with Kant: knowing it is ultimately impossible. Yet, Schopenhauer claims, reality *is* directly experienced by us through our Will. An examination of Schopenhauer's understanding of Will sheds light on his pessimism regarding human life and conduct.

Outline

I. We have looked at two models of philosophical guidance—that of Kant and that of Hegel—and at some of the specific advice that each has offered. Each model has a specific bearing on our present and has turned out to have unexpected consequences. Each also influences Arthur Schopenhauer.

   A. Kant's division of the world into appearance and reality is forwarded as a means of reconciling reason and faith.

      1. Recently, the progress of science has been thought by many to crowd faith out, or at least to make its presence less comfortable.

      2. The technological extension of knowledge that allows us to *do* with the world what we want suggests to us that we must actually know how things truly are.

      3. At one time, knowledge could mean obedience (conformity) to the nature of things, from which protection might arise and, hopefully, even transformation.

4. Knowledge has now come to mean instrumental power over things, the bending of them to human purposes.

5. Such progress and success have for many diminished both an interest in religion and a sense of its plausibility.

B. Kant promotes what might be termed "two-worldly" living. Based on the limitations of reason, science allows us to master appearances, and reality is reserved for us as an object of faith. At the same time, Kant promotes wonder through his conception of metaphysics as a natural disposition of the human soul.

1. Kant suggests that maybe we are two people: one who can wonder and the other who may be caught up in scientific investigation.

2. Kant remains concerned about origins and destinies.

3. Kant's concern with totalities leaves open questions regarding our place in the universe and the limits of the universe itself.

4. Kant reiterates that it is in the inescapable nature of our reason that we speculate.

II. Schopenhauer's importance arises out of his conception of our contact with reality. There is one place where Schopenhauer finds that contact direct and revelatory, *viz.*, through our own bodies. This finding is a significant departure in philosophy.

A. There are three strong aversions in philosophy regarding the body:

1. The Socratic-Platonic doctrine that the body is a prison or fortress from which we hope to escape;

2. The Augustinian complaint that the body leads to temptations and is a locus of desire; and

3. The Cartesian bifurcation of us into free, thoughtful minds problematically connected to materially determined bodies.

B. Schopenhauer gives a precise account of our direct experience of our bodies.

1. Knowledge of our bodies is "internal," nonrational, and nonsensory.

      a. Our actions and our "Will" are not causally related, but manifest the same thing, *viz.*, that which might be best referred to as energy.

      b. Regarding ourselves, this knowledge of our bodies is unique and noninferential. We just live it and are not its spectators.

    2. Our inner sense—applicable only to ourselves—gives direct knowledge of more than "acts of Will."

      a. Emotions, moods, desires, cravings, fears, and strivings are also made evident to us.

      b. Schopenhauer's pessimism is evident in his belief that these emotions and desires all are incessant, multiple, tangled, urgent, and often conflicting.

III. Schopenhauer's basic notion of reality is as "Will," but this is an unfortunate and misleading term.

  A. By Will, Schopenhauer has in mind a blind, rationally inaccessible force that is primitive energy itself.

    1. This energy manifests itself in and through everything and is best revealed, because only thinly veiled, in its manifestation in us.

    2. This energy is impersonal, insatiable, and its manifestation in us is a source of considerable suffering.

      a. Plato speaks about this energy in his writings.

      b. After desires and cravings are satisfied, there is a brief respite, but this is typically accompanied by a sense of boredom and emptiness.

      c. Unsatisfied desires are painful not to act upon, but seldom satisfied satisfactorily, and satisfaction often has unfortunate and painful consequences.

  B. Important comparative connections with the traditions of philosophy highlight Schopenhauer's thought.

    1. Kant's understanding of imagination and willpower has intriguing classical forbears in its own right.

    2. Plato's doctrine of the erotic comes closest to capturing Schopenhauer's intent.

    3. Hegel's emphasis on passion and spirit is nonetheless cognitive and rational in thrust. In contrast, Schopenhauer emphasizes the irrational.

IV. Schopenhauer's circumstances in life are claimed by some to illumine his fundamentally pessimistic outlook, which may have grown out of aspects of his temperament.

    A. His distant and dismissive relation to the official philosophical establishment is not to be taken lightly. It helps us to understand his outlook regarding philosophy as a guide to living. For instance, Schopenhauer felt in competition with Hegel.

    B. Schopenhauer has very complex and unfortunate attitudes toward women.

        1. Schopenhauer's life and writings regarding women were not well received.

        2. Schopenhauer had a complex relationship with his mother (a successful writer) as well as with Goethe.

    C. Schopenhauer's major work was not well received until several years before his death.

V. Schopenhauer believes that reason is impotent and stresses the importance of coming to terms with the Will.

    A. Reason is construed as the unwitting instrument of the Will.

        1. The outbreak of rational consciousness is but the provision of an arena for the Will's activity.

        2. History for Schopenhauer has no rational direction.

    B. The demands of the Will are insistent and insatiable.

        1. Schopenhauer was an agnostic.

        2. Schopenhauer turned toward Buddhism.

Essential Reading:

Bryan Magee, *The Philosophy of Schopenhauer*.

Arthur Schopenhauer, *The Will to Live*.

Supplementary Reading:

Rüdiger Safranski, *Schopenhauer and the Wild Years of Philosophy*.

Questions to Consider:

1. Why does Schopenhauer take Kant so seriously?

2. Should one's temperament be a factor in developing a philosophy of life?

Lecture Eight—Transcript
Schopenhauer's Pessimism

Reassurance on a journey such as we've been on is an important thing to offer. What we want to be able to think together is, "Yes, there's a restaurant ahead"—and by the way, we will be talking a little bit about food during the course of our time together today—and yes, that we may not find a place of true belonging, but we'll get a better understanding, at least of what the questions have been regarding the meaning of life and what philosophers have reflected on with respect to those questions. We've journeyed a long way together. Consider what we've reflected on with regard to Kant. Kant oddly claims that "the starry heavens above and the moral law" within fill him with ever increasing admiration and awe. But in the midst of that awe, regarding the "starry heavens above", which ultimately he says we can't fully know in their true nature, Kant does offer us the opportunity for a life in which we live with strict, moral principles. Some have said that Kant's notion of a staunch, austere reality actually makes the world safe for people that are very decent but very dull. That's one of the criticisms made of him.

That, in fact, partly engendered the Romantic reaction to Kant, and those Romantics who saw Kant as living in a world of austere morality—trying to suppress the passions—those Romantics emphasized imaginations. They emphasized trying to discover and find a way to express our inner nature and to find integrity and wholeness for the person and always in the back of their minds was not so much being decent and dull, certainly not being dull, but finding a way to be creative. Most recently, we had looked at Hegel who had given us a grand vision, a kind of bubble that Hegel saw the world living in and a wonderful, wonderful bubble that, for him, meant the end of history. The vision Hegel offered as to how to determine the meaning of life was that we could understand through our imagination we could recapitulate and see a narrative that told us the grand way in which history had unfolded. Though, we ourselves may not have made a specific contribution to that unfolding, we could nonetheless experience what it was like and we can say, "Yes, we've seen what history has meant."

Hegel also counseled as a young philosopher that we should live wholeheartedly, a passionate life, not an "austere, moral life," and we wouldn't necessarily have to be those creative, Romantic-type people who lived in *garrotes*, who embraced all kinds of odd things in the name of "creativity," we could live a passionate life in which we embrace conflicts, in which we live through them. Even if they were, for us, agonizing, we could embrace fully, life to its fullest, and even as the individuals we are, not perhaps, part of the whole of history and its meaning, we could have a full life.

Then as we saw, just a few lectures ago, Hegel talks about being "the solid citizen" and the notion of being just. Is that all he meant? A solid citizen gets powerful reactions against him. Let's continue on our journey. We've looked at two models of philosophical guidance and some of the specific advice they've offered and each has a bearing on the present on the time in which we now live and has turned out to have very unexpected consequences. Each has influenced the philosophy of Arthur Schopenhauer, whom we'll be talking about now.

Kant had divided the world into appearance and reality, and dividing the world into appearance and reality, he thought he'd brought faith and reason together. On the one hand, our reason could tell us the structure of how things appear and faith, though a very austere, moral faith as we saw it, could give us an idea of what reality is like. Now our concerns should not just be historical and concern what people once said; we should also look into the present. We know that progress of science in our time has been thought by many to crowd out faith. It has been thought by many to make a sense of faith less comfortable to hold onto.

That technological extension of knowledge that allows us to do with the world what we want, various medical advances and advances in physics, has suggested to us that we may know actually how the world is. Does that leave room for faith? That has been the question. Does the extension of knowledge put us in a position where, knowing more and more, no mystery remains? Once knowledge—or was it superstition?—could allow us to have a sense of conforming, maybe only through faith but conforming to the nature of things and out of that arose the notion that perhaps, if we conformed, if we had obedience and we had faith in a nature of things beyond us, well, maybe we would be protected. Maybe even if we had that connection with reality beyond us, perhaps only through faith or a strange wisdom we couldn't explain, we might be transformed.

It's different in our time. Knowledge has come to be construed as an instrument to give us power over things and the ability to bend them to human purposes. Such progress and success, in many minds, has diminished both religious interest and the sense of its plausibility of the religious consciousness. Has the room for faith been crowded out by recent developments in knowledge? Let's consider further. Kant promotes what can be thought of as a "two-worldly" living based in the limitations of reason, science allows us to master appearances, and reality is reserved for us as an object of faith. At the same time, Kant promotes wonder through his conception of our metaphysical nature. We can't have wonder about the nature of things, but he wants science to go forward, too.

What Kant suggests, then, is that maybe we are two people—on the one hand, a person who can wonder; on the other hand, a person who is caught up very much in scientific investigation. But in the midst of all that, Kant is very concerned about the origin and the destiny of the world in which we live. He is very concerned about our place in the totality of things and he leaves open questions regarding our place in the universe. He even leaves open questions about the limits of the universe itself. He reiterates that it is in the inescapable nature of our reason that we do, and we must, speculate.

So let's pause for just a moment and think about this. Let us pause and reflect. Kant had said that through reason and science, we know how things must appear, but he left room for a sense of faith and wonder. A sense that yes, there are "starry heavens above," that there's a moral law within, and somehow, out of that could come a sense of faith. But now, if we look into our present and the sense in which, in our present we could find meaning by, on the one hand, having rational investigation and on the other hand, beyond our rational investigation, a sense of wonder, in our time with the advance of science, it has seemed to be the case for some that the room for wonder has become less. Kant's notion that you could hold a life of science, and a life of "wonder and awe" in the universe together, has become for many, more difficult, far more difficult because science, supposedly, has extended further and made less and less of reality mysterious.

This is where Schopenhauer comes in to our consideration. Let us consider further. Schopenhauer's importance arises out of his conception of what our contact with reality actually is. There is one particular place that Schopenhauer finds our contact with reality direct and revelatory and that's through our own bodies. That's quite a significant departure in philosophy. There have been three very strong aversions in philosophy to regarding the body as the place of access to reality. We get from Socrates and Plato the notion that after all, our body is a kind of prison or a fortress, and ultimately we will hope to escape from it. From Augustine and all kinds of people in a more ascetic tradition, we get the notion that what the body does is lead us to temptations, and that our body is a place where desires team up, that distracts us and draw us away. Also, we find in philosophy a movement that begins in the 17th century, and what it has to do with is a bifurcation of us, a split in us between, on the one hand, our minds, our consciousness, with supposedly is very problematically connected with our materially determined bodies and the stress among these philosophers is to talk about the mind, not the body. To try to disconnect the mind from the body as far as reflecting on it is concerned and consider primarily, if not altogether, the mind.

Arthur Schopenhauer, a German philosopher who did most of his work in the 19th century, gives us a very precise account of our direct experience of our bodies. I'd like you to do something for me. Lift your arms up. Schopenhauer would tell us that in that very experience that you've just undergone, you've had a direct experience with reality and that our knowledge of reality, actually, is internal to us, it's non-rational, not irrational, but *non*-rational and it doesn't involve our senses. What Schopenhauer says is that we directly experience in our movements—we don't even think about our movements as we make them, we just make them—that very making of our movements is an experience in which we are one with reality. Now it is true that sometimes, not often but sometimes, we could say, "I'm going to get a glass," then I could walk across the room to get a glass. Then there's something such as my will involved, and then perhaps I'd walk across the room and pick up a glass. But normally, we just make movements and they are part of us, and for Schopenhauer, that's what reality really is.

That experience of reality that we have through our natural movements, through our experience with our bodies, might best be construed as energy. That which we are experiencing thereby is energy. Regarding ourselves, this knowledge of our bodies is unique, and we don't make inferences. It's non-inferential. We just have that experience. We live it. We're not spectators of it. We can look at things around us, but when I move around, I'm living, not simply looking. Schopenhauer gives us something that can be a cause of great concern and it will concern us greatly as we move forward because Schopenhauer says that not only in the movement of our body do we experience reality, but we have direct knowledge in what we do of a lot more than "acts of will."

What we experience directly as part of ourselves are our emotions, our moods, our desires, our cravings, our fears, and our strivings. They're also made evident to us. Now we verge on what I've mentioned before as Schopenhauer's pessimism. Because just as we've directly experienced the movement of our bodies in various ways, what we experience with our moods, our desires, our feelings, is that they are incessant. They're multiple, they're tangled, they're urgent, and often conflicting. Pause for a moment and think about this. Is it not the case that you directly experience all kinds of desires, urges, feelings, and emotions pulsing through you? Is this not something that is a very fundamental part of your experience? Schopenhauer says it is and it is our access to, and our experience of, what reality actually is.

Schopenhauer's notion is that reality is actually something that he calls the "will", but this is a very unfortunate and misleading term for Schopenhauer because, what Schopenhauer means by the word "will" is a blind, rationally inaccessible force that is a kind of primitive energy itself. This energy, he thinks, manifests itself in and through everything and is best revealed—because only thinly veiled—in its manifestation in us. He thinks that this energy is impersonal, insatiable, and in us it is a source of considerable suffering—a strange view of what reality is. So far, we have at least wanted to think of reality as something that is beyond normal things that might transform us. In Schopenhauer, reality, which we are in contact with, which we have an avenue to directly through our bodies, moods, feelings, and desires, is a pulsing something that in fact causes us, on Schopenhauer's view, great suffering.

Socrates talks to a man called Cephalus in one of Plato's *Dialogues*. Cephalus says what is important is actually to escape desires, to get beyond them, because if you can get beyond your desires, what in fact happens is you have tranquility, you have peace of mind, your desires are not viewed so much as opportunities but as distractions. This is the sort of view that Schopenhauer develops because, if we are to believe Schopenhauer, after you satisfy your cravings and desires, you have a brief respite, but typically then you become bored. Then you have, in your satiation, a sense of emptiness. But maybe that's the best story to be told. Schopenhauer says that unsatisfied desires, and most of our desires are unsatisfied, well, that's painful, because most of our desires are seldom satisfied satisfactorily and the satisfaction of desires, the acting on our emotions and feelings, often has very unfortunate and painful consequences.

There are kind of important, and I think, significant comparative connections with the tradition of philosophy that more or less puts Schopenhauer's philosophy and highlights in perspective. Kant had this notion of imagination and a notion of will and willpower and that has intriguing forbearers. We see in Plato the notion that deep within us is something Plato calls "*eros*," best understood as desire and that we have an underlying desire in us and that desire, whether we realize it or not, is always to be, and never *not* to be. Schopenhauer talks about something that looks a great deal like what Plato calls *eros* and understands the desire always to be and never *not* to be. Except for Schopenhauer, that underlying desire is actually a craving for satisfactions, many of which are not achieved, many of which cause pain, and those which are achieved lead to boredom.

Schopenhauer's view is nearly the opposite of the view that we see in Hegel. Hegel had that notion, has that notion, and offers that notion of the human spirit as a fusion of reason and imagination, reason and passion, and out of that comes considerable energy and celebration of life. Schopenhauer says, "No, what Hegel is talking about, well, that's grand to think, it's a very cozy notion. It's a way of celebrating one's self, perhaps." Perhaps—and we'll come to this—it's the sort of thing that a professor in Berlin with a chair in philosophy might want to say. But, for Schopenhauer, what is celebrated in spirit by Hegel, what is thought of in Plato is an underlying desire always to be and never not to be is really a pulsing, irrational force that wells up in us and we get glimpses of it and of its promise, which is very little and the way it burdens us, which is very great through our experience of our so-called "inner-lives" that we have access to.

Let's consider further. Schopenhauer holds a view that is, at best, pessimistic. If it is really true and the world is a world in which we are, yes, victims of our underlying desires, where they are a burden to us, where did that come from? Why should Schopenhauer have held such a view? Many say we may ask whether it's fair to Schopenhauer. We may even ask whether it's fair to any consideration of the meaning of life. Many ask whether it's caught up in Schopenhauer's own circumstances. There is a claim by many to illuminate why he's such a pessimist. They suggest his pessimism grew out of his underlying disposition. He had a very dismissive and dismissively distant relation to the official philosophical establishment, and I suppose we can't take that lightly.

It helps us to understand his outlook and how to regard philosophy, perhaps, as a guide to living. Schopenhauer felt himself in competition with Hegel. Very briefly, Schopenhauer had a position in Berlin teaching in the same institution as Hegel, and maybe even perversely, what Schopenhauer did was to schedule his courses at the very same time that Hegel's courses were offered. Nobody came to Schopenhauer's classes, or we have very little record of very many coming, and very few staying, while Hegel's classes were overloaded with people. Maybe that's human nature. If it turns out that someone is celebrating the life of the spirit, then the meaning of life is enjoying the spirit and understanding it. Maybe that draws a better crowd than an account of philosophy in which what you're doing is saying, "There's a force that wells up in you. It is always there. It gnaws at you. It is always victimizing you because it wants more and more. If you get what you want, you get bored. If you get what you want it might be a painful experience, but usually you don't get what you want."

We'll have to say—it's another controversial point—that, at very best, Schopenhauer has very complex and, in fact, unfortunate attitudes about women, and it comes through in his writings. For one thing, he says women shouldn't be allowed in the theatre. That's because they wouldn't understand what was going on there. He also says that women really are seductresses. "You've got to be careful about women because they're always out to make you the father of their children. That's their goal in life." Schopenhauer does give them considerable credit as mothers. He says they're very good with children, but the reason he says they're very good with children is because they're children themselves and never become more than that.

Schopenhauer's mother was a very, very close and intellectual friend with Goethe, the philosopher, political theorist, scientist and writer. At one point, Schopenhauer's mother wrote her son a letter and said, "Get lost." Well, she didn't quite put it that way. She happened to be in Weimar, Germany, where Goethe and some of the celebrated figures of the day were, and she was writing popular things that were selling. Well, Schopenhauer came around for a while but he got on his mother's nerves. He got in the way of her life there and she said, "I hope I never have to see you again."

Notice that I've just mentioned that she was a popular writer. What I haven't mentioned, and that I've saved for this moment to tell you, is that Schopenhauer published one major work in 1818. It was called, *The World as Will and Idea*. Seeing nobody bought it or read it, Schopenhauer didn't write for decades because he said, "I've said how things are in that work. Why should I write something more? I've said how things are and if people aren't going to listen to it, too bad." Here is Schopenhauer's mother, a very popular writer who has told him that he is irksome and she just wishes he was completely out of her life. He's written a book nobody reads. He ends up living in Frankfurt, Germany, doing no more writing for a long time.

Let me move us slightly now toward the point of turn. Schopenhauer believes that reason is important and stresses the importance of coming to terms with those underlying energies that pulse through us. Reason, which Kant and Hegel celebrated—Schopenhauer says it's a blind, unwitting instrument of this underlying energy—this thing that Schopenhauer calls "the will," and Schopenhauer actually says that our rational consciousness is just kind of an arena that gets created by the will for the will's activity. Schopenhauer tells us that history doesn't have a rational direction. History is just things happening and they happen because this will that we experience through us, but is at work everywhere, just keeps pulsing to express itself and to satisfy itself.

About ultimate reality, Schopenhauer is very agnostic. He makes virtually no claims about ultimate reality. He says things of this sort—thousands of years passed before any of us were born, likely an eternity is going to pass after we die and we discover ourselves. Here in the world, we've got these fancy philosophical types who are telling us we can celebrate the human spirit. They are telling us that we can learn to conquer our desires through reason. They tell us that we can be creative spirits and outsiders, remove ourselves from the urban, the industrial, we can learn to express ourselves and be creative. That's all fine and good, and they talk about the difference between the mind and the body. That's all find and good, but just let yourself experience your life. Come down off the high pedestal of professional philosophy and think about how you want food, want experience, want excitement. Sometimes it comes to you, sometimes it doesn't. When your desires are met, they're usually not met comfortably. Most of your desires aren't met at all. So you suffer. You're always in a state of tension because of suffering, because of desire.

As we'll look at a little further in our next lecture, Schopenhauer comes to wonder whether Buddhism has something to offer to our human predicament of being caught up in desires that are always pressing on us and always haunting us. Schopenhauer may have been the first major philosophical thinker to bring Buddhist thinking to the West, a kind of thinking that's more concerned to separate us from our desires than to satisfy them. Well, perhaps that's an avenue we can look into, but if Schopenhauer's account of how the world is, is right, what does he think we can do? This pessimistic account of reality is not reason, but a pulsing, underlying energy that victimizes us, what are our options? How might we find a cure? What does Schopenhauer think we can do?

Lecture Nine
Schopenhauer's Remedies

Scope:

Optimally, a guide to living delivers us not only from something but also for or to something. The latter is lacking in Schopenhauer. In the end there is nothing. Philosophy can only diagnose. It can suggest partial alleviations but not provide them, according to Schopenhauer. As with Marx, solutions must come from elsewhere. Schopenhauer offers four routings. The first involves assuming a disengaged, aesthetic attitude. A second requires the recognition that we humans are all the victims of the same inexorable agonies. Out of this recognition a consoling sympathy might arise. A third option is to pay special heed to certain forms of music as a means of assuaging the Will. Finally, Schopenhauer counsels a losing of the Will to live and, in this counsel, he claims to touch base with the depths of Buddhism. We will consider the significance of this claim.

Outline

I. Under the influence of the axial model, philosophy as a guide to living has often been concerned with the notion of deliverance, a deliverance from the human "predicament."

    A. Because philosophy has primarily been rationalistic and emphasized the benefits of thought, the philosophical concern has mostly been with the predicament of ignorance.

        1. Often this has involved a distinction between a lower and a higher nature possessed by human beings.

        2. Typically, the lower nature is viewed either as bad in itself or, less negatively, as tending to distract us from the pursuit of higher things.

        3. As predecessors to Schopenhauer, both Kant and Hegel provide illustrations of this notion of deliverance.

            a. Kant's notion of a rational moral life subsumes desires and puts the Will at the service of reason.

            b. Hegel distinguishes between our ordinary life in the world and our philosophical comprehension of the world.

    c. Both conceptions can be derived from a faculty of psychology found in Plato.

  B. In Schopenhauer, whose views become quite influential, knowledge that overcomes ignorance regarding our human situation is not enough, for knowledge alone cannot bring about deliverance.

    1. Schopenhauer conceives knowledge to be the largely unwitting tool of the activities of the Will, the pulsing energy within us.

    2. Knowledge is controlled by and does not itself control the Will.

    3. Strictly speaking, knowledge is limited to appearances and offers explanations that do not reach reality.

    4. Schopenhauer's own wisdom regarding life is instructively problematic.

  C. Schopenhauer's "world"—which he construes as appearance—is understood materialistically. But Schopenhauer claims the world could not be material.

    1. Issues regarding causality and the presence of "forces" in nature make a materialist account unviable.

    2. Schopenhauer's basic categories (space, time, causality, and motivation) are limited to "appearances."

    3. Schopenhauer, in some respects, anticipates more contemporary physics and, in other respects, Sigmund Freud.

II. For Schopenhauer, reality (the Will) is something to be escaped, not something to be embraced. There are four methods by which this escape might be sought.

  A. Escape from the destructive ravages of the Will is made necessary by Schopenhauer's account of its nature.

    1. The Will's activities are not historically progressive.

    2. The Will is insatiable and uncontrollable.

  B. The four methods of escape from the influence of the Will each have limitations.

    1. *Aesthetic contemplation* is one avenue, but its effectiveness is temporary.

    a. The spectatorial nature of contemplation diverts us from those urgent drives at the heart of the Will's dynamics.

    b. The energy required to sustain the contemplative is insufficient to the task, however.

    c. The notions of disengagement and "getting one's mind on other things" illustrate Schopenhauer's notion of the aesthetic.

2. The *cultivation of sympathy* for one's fellow beings is another avenue of escape, but its effectiveness is also temporary.

    a. Sympathy involves the recognition that each individual is a manifestation of Will and thus suffers the same agonies as all others.

    b. Sympathy may engender a noncompetitive quietism that assuages the Will's drives.

3. *Music* has a special capacity to capture the rhythms of the Will in an assuaging way.

    a. Schopenhauer believes that music is the noumenal expressing itself through us.

    b. One major power that music has is to circumvent our intellects and speak to us in a language of its own that makes us more at one with ourselves.

    c. This idea captivated the great German composer, Richard Wagner, who read Schopenhauer.

    d. Music is a means of engendering wants, playing them out, and then bringing them to closure and satisfaction.

4. The best, though most challenging, strategy would be *to lose the "Will to live,"* to reach a condition of quiescence where our individual Wills do not toss and turn us.

    a. The loss of the Will to live is not the same as the desire to commit suicide.

    b. Suicide would itself be an act of Will.

III. Schopenhauer brings a strongly negative and pessimistic element into the European philosophical scene, which tempers the rationalism and the optimism of the Enlightenment and of Hegel. Utopian hopes begin to recede.

    A. A subterranean, nonrational reality not only comes strongly forward but begins to dominate.

    B. The notion of a Higher Realm, beyond or after this one, is rejected.

    C. The parallels with Eastern philosophy, particularly Buddhism, are strong and suggest that peace of mind and disengagement from the painful cycle of desire—not progress—are the ultimate goals.

Essential Reading:

Bryan Magee, *The Philosophy of Schopenhauer.*

Arthur Schopenhauer, *The Will to Live.*

Supplementary Reading:

Bryan Magee, *Wagner and Philosophy.*

Irvin Yalom, *The Schopenhauer Cure.*

Questions to Consider:

1. Do Schopenhauer's remedies strike you as realistic?

2. Is Schopenhauer's understanding of the Will too pessimistic?

Lecture Nine—Transcript
Schopenhauer's Remedies

As we've seen in our last time together, if we're to believe Schopenhauer, life isn't exactly something to be celebrated. We are in fact, victims of life, and if you're going to talk about the "human predicament", that predicament is that we're living at all and that actually, it would have been best if we'd never been born. It's not as if there's a meaning to life. We may take a journey in order to find it and in finding it we will be transformed. If we look into the heart of Schopenhauer's thought, there is no meaning to life, but here we are anyway and it's a balance a good thing if we don't linger here terribly long. The meaning of life is partly the discovery that there is no meaning to our lives and that perhaps the best thing is an exit.

Speaking simply, what an awful mess to be in! What a terrible situation! If there ever was pessimism, this is it. This is Schopenhauer's pessimism. Now, under the axial model of philosophy that we've looked at as a guide to living, where we're on a journey and we're trying to find our way to reality, we have a notion of deliverance, a deliverance from the human predicament. That deliverance is often understood as escaping ignorance, but maybe the deliverance needs to be something else. Now, because philosophy has primarily been rational and primarily emphasized the benefits of thought, usually the philosophical concern has been with that very predicament of ignorance. It's thought by many that what's involved is a distinction between our lower natures and our higher natures, and that we have both lower and higher natures. Typically, our lower nature is viewed either as bad in itself or, less negatively, as tending to distract us from the things that matter, the things that could transform us.

Predecessors to Schopenhauer, for instance, both Kant and Hegel, in a way provide accounts of a kind of deliverance we might have from ignorance and a transformation of our lives to a higher level. Remember that Kant says there could be a rational, moral life. There could be a life in which in fact we would find our duty, we would act under the proper motives, we would live under the rational morality, we would keep our desires subsumed and in order, and that would relieve us of the dangers and the distractions of desire, and allow us better to have awe and wonder, and think of questions—though we can't answer them—nonetheless, questions that'd make us fully human to ask.

Hegel distinguishes between our ordinary life in the world and our philosophical comprehension of the world, and what Hegel thinks is that we are at a higher level. We have overcome ignorance and the confusion and the loud noise and roar of an often kind of confusing history. If we could understand a narrative story that tells why history has come where it has, what our place can be in it and what history means. So in both cases—with Kant, a rational morality that might have rationally religious consequences, with Hegel, a comprehension of the journey of the human spirit—we do have the notion of deliverance from ignorance and a movement toward maybe at least an elevating insight, maybe not necessarily a transforming one. Both of these conceptions, whether Kant's or Hegel's, actually derive from a kind of psychology found in Plato where we have, at the highest level, reason; then we have our will and our willpower, and beneath that we have our desires. In the best of worlds, reason rules, it guides the will and our will takes care of, controls, and moderates our desires.

It's different in Schopenhauer. In Schopenhauer—and we're going to see this, his views do become terribly influential—knowledge that overcomes ignorance regarding our human situation is not enough. We can know all the sorts of things he's already told us that we've talked about in the previous lecture, but that knowledge in itself won't be enough to have. It won't get the job done and that's even further pessimism. Schopenhauer, as we know, has talked about how there's this pulsing desire, this energy craving satisfaction in us, and now that we know that, what do we do? Schopenhauer says knowing this, as he says he's told us, isn't enough. It isn't going to solve the problem. What Schopenhauer does tell us is that when you come right down to it, knowledge is just simply the unwitting tool of the activities of the will, of the activities of this pulsing energy within us.

I think there's a very nice way to illustrate this. It comes from the novel that I believe won the National Book Award. The novel is *From Here to Eternity* and its author is James Jones. Not only did I read the novel but also I saw the movie and, in my era, it was a different set of actors that played in it. But in any case, if you look closely at that novel, there's a particular scene that I think is very revealing, and you could almost say it's out of Schopenhauer. A sergeant comes to the home of the captain of the base. The captain of the base is not home, but in that home is the captain's wife. The captain's wife and the sergeant sit and chat with each other, and actually, it's a fairly sophisticated conversation. Well, it's complicated anyway, because they're talking about—guess what?—philosophy. You can almost say that through philosophy they're talking about what the meaning of life might be. It doesn't go quite that far, but that element is in it. Well, at one point, the wife of the captain starts to take off her clothes and she says to the sergeant, "Isn't this really what our conversation is about? All this fancy talk we've been having about philosophy and ideas, isn't this really what is going on between us?" Well, I won't go any further in the story except to tell you it might be saved from an X rating because what happens is they hear the crunch of gravel in the driveway as the captain has come back—full stop. The sergeant leaves and the rest is history.

What Schopenhauer would have said about this is, "Ah, nearly a perfect model of what human life is like." There are these underlying magnetisms, these underlying desires. It's awkward for us to talk about them, but they're always there. We often live in a fancy world of ideas. We get articulate. We talk about grand things. We get analytical. We get reflective, but beneath it all we all know that, every day in every part of our lives—and there wouldn't necessarily have to be sexual parts—every time we pass a particular restaurant—I won't name any here—or any particular place to get coffee, or any particular place where a desire of ours might be satisfied, what happens? What happens is that we're reminded that these are the sorts of desires and things that are us, and if we could admit it to ourselves, rule us.

Let's consider further. Schopenhauer thinks knowledge is controlled by and does not itself control the will. Strictly speaking, he thinks knowledge, as Kant did, is restricted to appearances and offers explanations that do not reach reality. Schopenhauer does claim to have a kind of wisdom regarding human life, though he says knowledge isn't the cure. Schopenhauer isn't going to leave us absolutely at sea, though he does have some solutions, some remedies. If life is the disease, and importantly, Schopenhauer thinks it is, Schopenhauer often speaks and often offers cures or a cure. He says that the world that we experience, we understand materialistically. But he claims that the world couldn't be a material world. There has to be something behind it. He says if you think about causality, if you think about the presence of "forces" in nature, a material account will finally not add up. But he doesn't go into that in any great detail. He tells us that there are basic categories our minds have to use—we have to think of things as being in space, we have to think about them as being in time, we have to use causal notions, we think of inner motivations. But those categories only give us the appearance of things, never their underlying reality.

Now in some ways, in some of the things that Schopenhauer is saying, he anticipates some developments in contemporary science, and with respect to what he says about the "agony" of what is the deepest in us, in some ways he anticipates some things that are said by the great psychoanalyst Sigmund Freud, who we'll be talking about in a later lecture.

We might pause for a moment just to realize that Schopenhauer leaves us in fundamental, underlying dilemmas. We know appearance, but it couldn't be reality. Our own experience of our secret inner life, secret in a sense of that it would probably embarrass us to talk about it, is really the experience of reality. Well, what to do? How to get some kind cure for what could almost be called the disease of living? Well, let's consider this one further. Let's see where he can take us. He says this will, this underlying energy, is something to be escaped. It's not something to be embraced. He thinks there are four methods we might use in order to escape it.

We need to escape the destructive ravages of the will because of the very account Schopenhauer has given us of its nature. He says this will is not progressive. It isn't, as in Hegel, that there is this "grand journey of the spirit" going through stages. As we know, Hegel thought that by the 19th century, "Happy, happy!" and for us even more so. All these stages have been gone through and we can celebrate them. Our imagination can allow us to recapitulate them. We can enjoy them. We can say we've arrived. Oh no. Schopenhauer says history really isn't going anywhere. All of the scientific and technological progress there ever could be—we're not going anywhere. Here we are. It's too bad that we're here. But we're not going anywhere in the sense of the progress of history.

Schopenhauer also says that this underlying energy, which he calls "the will," as I've said before is insatiable. Every satisfaction leaves you probably temporarily satisfied, then bored, and then the desire comes back. Or maybe you don't get the satisfaction that you need or that you want and there couldn't even be an unexpectedly painful satisfaction. So in a way, what Schopenhauer's saying is, our life is a life of deep, agonizing frustration. The meaning of life, no meaning, the pursuit of a meaning of life, well our pursuits should be delivered from the human "predicament". That predicament again, is that here we are. The predicament is not that we don't know enough. The predicament is that we live at all.

I hope by now you've got some sense of why I say Schopenhauer is a pretty pessimistic guy. Well, he does offer four methods of escape from this influence of pulsing energy we call "the will," and as we'll see, each has to a certain degree, significant limitations. How to be delivered from our pulsing energy that is the depth of us? How to get beyond it? Realizing that's what the pulsing course of history is. Well, the first of the solutions Schopenhauer suggests is what we might call aesthetic contemplation—though he tells us that aesthetic contemplation…well, its effectiveness is pretty temporary. For example, we can get our mind off things, say, by seeing a movie. Well, there weren't movies, of course, in Schopenhauer's day but kinds of examples he might give would be looking at paintings. That maybe if we get absorbed in something, we'll at least temporarily get our minds off the kind of underlying agony that is the constant companion of our lives. But he says that this "spectatorial" nature of contemplation, which diverts us from our underlying, urgent drives and is the heart of the will's dynamics, is kind of fleeting; you can't sustain it. The energy required to sustain a contemplative life of aesthetic contemplation is kind of insufficient. It is insufficient to the task. The notions of disengagement and "getting one's mind off one's real life" illustrate what he means by the aesthetic but he tells us in the same breath it doesn't get the job done. But try it anyway. It might be helpful for a while.

The second suggestion Schopenhauer makes is the cultivation of sympathy for one's fellow beings. That could be another avenue of escape, but he says its effectiveness is also temporary. It is Schopenhauer's view that we might recognize that each individual, not just me, you, anyone you know, is an expression, an instance of this pulsing energy, this craving that is the will. That means that all of us suffer as manifestations of this. We suffer the same agonies, and maybe realizing that, having some sympathy for the fact we're all together in this and that it's an awful thing to be in, but that we're in it together and we might as well realize, actually, that we're all suffering. Schopenhauer thinks that that will also in a way, however temporarily, alleviate this sense of underlying agony of desires felt, denied, desires we tried to hide from ourselves, desires that we live with and don't know what to do with— maybe a sense of sympathy that that's everybody's situation might be a partial alleviation. Not a cure, but at least something that temporarily will help us along and perhaps that will engender a kind of noncompetitive quietism that will temporarily assuage this gnawing desirous nature that we have.

It's a large moment in the history of development in European thought when Schopenhauer tells us the third avenue. The first being aesthetic contemplation, fleeting, but gets our mind off things, the second being sympathy, knowledge that we're all stuck. We're all in it together. We all suffer. Well, the third is music. He thinks that music has a special capacity to capture the rhythms of our underlying will, the rhythms of this pulsing energy within us— that this music, is the right sort of music we listen to in the right way might assuage the agonies of our will. What Schopenhauer actually believes is that music is noumenal. That's the old word that we looked at before from Kant. It means that music puts us in touch with reality itself and as we fuse with music, we experience reality itself through us. But, in an assuaging way, it calms us, or can calm us. A major power that music has is to circumvent our intellects. Music for Schopenhauer is not meant to make us know anything. It's to get us away from thinking about anything, much less trying to know something. He thinks that music speaks in a language that can and does put us more at one with ourselves. I must say it probably gives away my age that a lot of the music I listen to myself doesn't exactly make me one with myself, but, well, I won't go very far into that.

A very famous German composer of the 19th century was Richard Wagner. He's probably known a great deal for various operas that he wrote. Now it turned out that Wagner read Schopenhauer's philosophy. Remember that I said before that *The World as Will and Representation* was written by Schopenhauer in 1818. I told you that very few people read it and paid attention to it, but Wagner did and was enthralled by it. We can guess why, because it said that music can put us in touch with reality itself, and even if you understand reality to be this pulsing energy that agonizes its craving way through us, even if you understand it in that way, music can assuage that. Music can calm that and of course—and we're going to look at this a little later when we're together—Wagner thought, yes, his music did that. Schopenhauer was right about what music could do and Wagner thought that Wagner's own music accomplished that.

Schopenhauer also thought less, I suppose in a deep level that music was a way of engendering in us also some wants, playing them out and then bringing them to closure and satisfaction. He had the idea that music could also not just calm us, but captures rhythms in the underlying will that is our nature. Capturing those rhythms, in some way, brings a more rhythmic quality to our living, which would make it less brutally a matter of cravings and desires and what to do about them.

But it turns out that the very best, though the most challenging strategy that Schopenhauer puts before us is the idea—hold your breath now, take a breath—that the best we might do is lose the will to live. Oh my! Schopenhauer thinks perhaps the best of all the remedies for the disease called life and its agonies would be to reach a condition of quiescence, a certain kind of mellow and benign passivity, where our individual wills do not toss and turn us anymore—that we, in a way, don't allow anything to matter to us, even our very selves. It's his view that the loss of the will to live is not the same as the desire to commit suicide. For, maybe only a philosopher can say this—philosophers say such strange things—suicide, he says, would be an act of will. Well, we have to scratch our heads. If life is such a mess, such an agony, why does it have to be the case that if we commit suicide, which would put us out of our agony, it would be the wrong thing to do, because that would be giving into the will and acting on it. I won't pursue that any further other than to tell you that, for Schopenhauer, no, it isn't that you would ever commit suicide. What you would do is reach that benign and mellow point where things didn't matter anymore, even yourself. If even you, yourself, didn't matter anymore, it wouldn't be an important thing to do even to commit suicide, because even committing suicide wouldn't matter.

Let's pause for a moment now and consider, then, where we stand. This is an odd place to be. We can have knowledge of something called the human "predicament," but we want to pause and consider what it means. The human predicament is that we are victims of life. Life itself is the disease and we need a cure from that disease. and all the knowledge in the world won't bring about the cure.

Let's consider further. Schopenhauer brings a very strongly negative and pessimistic element into the European philosophical thinking. He tempers the rationalism in the celebration of the spirit and the optimism of the 18th century Enlightenment. He tempers the enthusiasm of Hegel and the idea that we can be spectators and even in small ways, participants, in the grand story of history. He tempers anything like a utopian hope, not only for the world but also for any one of us living our individual lives. What he gives us is a subterranean, painfully hidden, or maybe even more painfully not hidden, non-rational reality that is us, that is our core and that, for Schopenhauer, is what the issue and what the predicament of life is. The notion of a higher realm, beyond or after this one, is rejected. That isn't what Schopenhauer thinks would be there. He's very agnostic about it. He doesn't give it very much thought. The parallels with Eastern philosophy, with Buddhism, are quite strong and they suggest that the meaning of life—if we can say there is one—is to achieve peace of mind. A kind of disengagement from the cycle or the painful rhythms of desire, satisfaction of desire, failure to satisfy desire, failure to admit that when all is said and done, what we don't really think finally matters as knowledge. What we do think that finally matters is getting our desires satisfied and life continues to tell us it's a painful enterprise and it doesn't very often work out.

Well, I mentioned before, Schopenhauer is very taken with Buddhist doctrines. As I said before, he probably was the major influential figure who brought Buddhist thinking to the West in a way that made it spread. If we reflect for just a minute on what that thinking tells us and the message that it gives us, what is it? It's that life is suffering and to be alive is suffering. It's the message that suffering is brought about by desire and desire does have a cure and the cure is no longer to be attached. Therefore, as we move toward the end of our consideration of Schopenhauer, what we have to reflect on most centrally is that for Schopenhauer, it is our own inner desires—that our reality itself manifesting itself through us, it is those desires that we must lose our attachment to. We must become, in a mellow and benign way, no longer caring, no longer concerned—because all that does is bring hurt and bring pain. So it is a disengagement Schopenhauer recommends. It is a sense that there is no meaning of life but here we are and we can find a way to come to terms, to become mellow, to become no longer involved, not only in questions about the meaning of life but we can become less concerned about the world itself.

Well, we need now to turn our attention in a different direction, nearly the opposite from Schopenhauer, because, as we return to talk to each other again, we're going to be looking at someone who plunges very directly into a consideration of the world, the so-called "real world," and that thinker is Karl Marx.

Lecture Ten
Alienation in Marx

Scope:

A guide to living must understand the nature of that Self whose life will be led. Hegel understands this Self socially, institutionally, and individually. Controversially, Hegel understands us to stand in a complex relation to ourselves. It forms us, but does so in significant measure through the sociopolitical institutions in which we find ourselves embedded. Our self-relatedness does not take place in a vacuum, and, if those societal arrangements that form the fabric of our self-relatedness are changed, we ourselves are very essentially changed as well.

For Karl Marx (1818–1883) it is not our reason, but socioeconomic forces that constitute our basic relation with the world. He believes that not thought, but the *concrete*, the work activities we engage in, reveal, determine, and distort our natures.

Outline

I. Guidance in living can be understood as seeking some form of escape from the world or as seeking conquest of or reconciliation with the world. In any of these alternatives, the world we find ourselves in must be understood for what it is.

    A. Influencing Marx greatly, not only negatively but positively, Hegel understands our very human natures—thus our identities—to be bound up in sociopolitical and economic circumstances.

        1. The early Hegel, a positive influence on Marx, sees such circumstances as often in need of dramatic alteration (revolution). He writes about the three outcomes of such an alteration:

            a. It might result in chaos.

            b. It might result in even worse circumstances.

            c. It might result in better circumstances.

2. The later Hegel, a very negative influence on Marx, celebrates the virtues of Prussian society and claims that its structures are supportive of our human identity and require no essential alteration.

B. Marx believes that the institutional arrangements of the world in which he finds himself do not reflect and respond to human need nor to the potential of human nature. Thus, Hegel's celebration of such arrangements enrages Marx.

    1. Marx sees the dynamic and courageous spirit of the early Hegel giving way to a self-serving, complacent, and highly inequitable conservatism.

    2. Marx calls *alienation* the circumstance in which one does not find oneself acknowledged in and through the institutional arrangements that are supposed to mirror and speak to one.

    3. Alienation can be understood as a disconnection with something to which you belong—and which is meant to be supportive of you. Marx finds our primary disconnection, and thus alienation, in the socioeconomic circumstances and dynamics in which a person is enmeshed.

II. Philosophers often take our basic relation to the world to be the most revealing indicator of our own nature and of the world's most basic features.

A. Hegel understands this pivotal relation to be by means of thought.

    1. Hegel confirms the Western valuing of rational comprehension as our highest capacity. In both the Greeks and Hegel, it is importantly spectatorial.

    2. Hegel directs such knowledge toward the concrete, social, and cultural world of his time, not beyond it.

    3. Hegel believes his current world incorporates the completion of history itself.

    4. Hegel understands knowing as a continuing recapitulation and appropriation of what is already known in the full richness of its content.

5. The world so revealed is rich in features but remains pervasively an object of rational comprehension.

B. Marx understands our most crucial and revelatory relation to the world to be through work (or labor). We have no adequate term for exactly what Marx has in mind, though we understand it quite well from our ordinary experience.

1. Concrete, practical engagement in the world expresses most fundamentally our own natures as agents unavoidably and constitutively involved in cooperatively productive activities.

2. Such engagement reveals as well a malleable world of socioeconomic relations and forces into which the natural world is drawn. The ideas and cultural elements found in these circumstances are derivative from this matrix of relations and forces.

III. Marx's diagnostic understanding of our alienation involves at least three circumstances in which a separation of ourselves from our true underlying nature occurs.

A. In the positive, nonalienated circumstance, the "something" that results from a person's productive activity is made in the manner that its "author" chooses to make it, and that producer is entitled to dispose of it in the manner in which he or she chooses.

1. If this occurs, the agent involved is productively free and self-determining.

2. Marx claims that the result—the "product" involved—can then be construed as an essential expression of its producer. It is importantly a dimension of that person himself or herself.

3. The activities involved and results of these activities—the products—are understood by Marx to enter into the very constitution of the person who is their author. Through such activities, people become who they really are, much more so than through the ideas or thoughts that these people might happen to have. Marx construes these ideas and thoughts as mere epiphenomena, impotent results of underlying activities, but not contributors to these activities—in other words, only effects not causes.

B. In the positive, nonalienated circumstance, the productive agent's time is his or her own and is subject only to the timing and partitionings of time that are of that agent's own choosing.

   1. Even as early as the Stoics, we have the notion that our relation to our own time is most intimate, and to hypothecate our time is essentially to impoverish ourselves.

   2. Two essential questions arise regarding our time.

      a. Does it belong to us or to someone else?

      b. Does it belong to us, or do we belong to *it*?

   3. There is an important experiential distinction between clock and "existential" time. The first externalizes us. The latter is potentially restorative.

   4. The Stoic Seneca says that, among all of our possessions, time is the most precious, and, paradoxically, we are always giving it to others.

   5. Marx says that our time must be our own, not sold to others. He finds the world exploitative, enslaving people who are forced to sell their time to others.

C. In the positive, nonalienated circumstance that Marx extols, the relations that humans sustain with each other are concrete, existential relations that are fully human, involving a wide range of aspects.

   1. Marx claims that such relations enter into our very nature and that not the least of them is the relation of man and woman.

2. Marx reacts critically to a matrix of human relations that sorts them out primarily in economic terms, for example, buyer and seller, economic competitors, and employer and employee.

Essential Reading

Karl Marx, *The Marx-Engels Reader*.

———, *Writings of the Young Marx on Philosophy and Society*.

Supplementary Reading:

Eric Fromm, *Marx's Concept of Man*.

Questions to Consider:

1. How does Marx believe that he departs from Hegel and prior philosophical thought?

2. To what degree has Marx been influenced by Hegel?

3. What are the basic elements of reality for Marx?

Lecture Ten—Transcript
Alienation in Marx

One of the major lines that we would have to see threading its way through Western philosophy is that ideas matter. If we were going to talk about the meaning of life, the avenue to discovering that meaning would be through ideas. For the Greeks, the ideas were of the sort that, as spectators, we would come to contemplate, and that might raise us beyond the normal world as we understand it. But from the Greeks—and religions to the West have added to this and complimented it and even become rivals to it—it's the idea that not only do ideas matter, but the meaning of life, in an important way, is literal or metaphorical, found beyond this world. By the time we come to Hegel, history matters utterly. The history Hegel talks about is a grand, intellectual odyssey, and we are both in it but can also tell a story about it that allows us to appreciate that grand, intellectual odyssey, that journey of history. Of course, whether it's the Greeks or whether it is Hegel, a grand vision is presented.

Now again, in our last two lectures, we've looked at a great alternative to that. Or is it an abysmal one, a very pessimistic one, where ideas do not finally matter because life itself does not matter? We saw through Schopenhauer the idea that it is disengagement from the world and from allowing life to agonize us that constitutes what meaning life might have for us. but let's now consider—guidance in living, as philosophy might hope to provide it, can be understood as seeking some form of escape from the world or as seeking conquest of or reconciliation with the world. In any of these alternatives, the world we find ourselves in must be understood for what it is.

Now, influencing Karl Marx, a German philosopher who lived from 1818 to 1883, and actually lived most of his adult life in London, and influencing him greatly, not only negatively but also positively, was how Hegel understood our very human natures, and how Hegel understood that nature to be bound up in socio-political and economic circumstances. The early Hegel, the exciting Hegel whom we've talked about before, who wrote *The Phenomenology of Spirit* in 1807, had a very positive influence on Marx. This Hegel saw such circumstances often in need of a very, very, dramatic alteration. In fact, we talked about that in relation to a famous passage in Hegel, which is referred to and written as *Freedom and Terror*. It involves, in this early Hegel, who so influenced Karl Marx, three possible outcomes.

One outcome was this—that there could be, if our legitimate needs weren't met, the requirement for a kind of revolution. But an outcome of that revolution might well be that we have nothing but chaos in the wake of a radical revolutionary change. Another outcome that Hegel thought was possible if we sought our freedom through radically overturning things was that we might come into a situation that was worse, not better. A third outcome—and the one that mattered most to this early Marx—was that we would reach a situation, if we took the revolutionary step, where circumstances would be better. The early Hegel thinking at least three outcomes were possible—a revolution ending in chaos, a revolution ending in a worse situation, and a revolution ending in a better situation—is funny. This Hegel thought that the French Revolution was the right thing to have done. He said it had many terrifying consequences but we learned a lot from it. And Hegel actually felt that the book he wrote, *The Phenomenology of Spirit,* reflected on and figured out what that Revolution meant and could understand what the right outcome would look at and look like, whether the French had specifically reached that outcome or not. So this early Hegel—the Hegel who thought revolution was, in a way, a very, very dangerous thing to undertake but at the same time filled with possibilities—very much enchanted and inspired Marx.

Let's consider further because something happens with the work of Hegel. That is the work of a later Hegel, about 20 years later, who is a very negative influence on Marx. He is a negative influence because this Hegel celebrates the virtues of Prussian society and claimed that the structures of Prussian society were supportive of our human identity and required no essential alteration. If the early Hegel thought revolution was a very precarious undertaking but might need to be done, the later Hegel thought that there was no need. There could be peace and ill reform. Everything was fine. Now, famously it's said that if Hegel found in middle class Prussian society a heaven in the 1820s, Marx found in it a hell.

Marx believes that the institutional arrangements of the world in which we find ourselves often—and this was the thought Marx had in his time—do not reflect, do not respond to human need, and they don't speak to the potential of our human nature. Thus, Hegel's later philosophy of the 1820s, which said that society as it was now constituted was supportive, and spoke to, acknowledged and recognized the rational, essential nature of human beings, enraged Marx. To him that was just simply false. It was very cozy. It was very conservative. It was just awful.

Marx saw the dynamic and courageous spirit of the early Hegel giving way to a self-serving, smug, complacent and highly inequitable conservatism. The circumstance in which one does not find oneself acknowledged, recognized, in and through institutional arrangements—that circumstance, in which you are supposed to be mirrored, acknowledged and recognized but you're not—Marx refers to as alienation. Marx thought that we lived, if we were in Marx's time, in a very alienated world where the institutions and circumstances around us do not speak to us, do not recognize us, do not acknowledge us.

How to understand alienation? Perhaps it's best understood as follows. We are alienated if we are disconnected from some circumstances, from something to which, in an important way, we belong, which is meant to be supportive of us, and though we are meant to belong, and that is meant to be supportive of us, if it doesn't support us, then we are in a condition of alienation. It is essential to us that somehow we are disconnected. It does not speak to us. It does not nurture, sustain and support us. Yet we need it. If that's the circumstance, we are alienated, and Marx thought that we lived in a state of alienation. The socioeconomic circumstances and dynamics in which a person is enmeshed, Marx thought, were often circumstances that were, in a sense, alienating.

Philosophers often take our basic relation to the world to be the most revealing and the most important indicator of our own nature and of the world's most basic features. Now, as we know, Hegel and Kant, in the grand Western rational tradition, understand our pivotal relation to the world to be in terms of thought. After all, Hegel confirms the Western valuing of rational comprehension as our highest capacity. In both the Greeks and Hegel, it is importantly "spectatorial", though Hegel directs such knowledge toward the concrete, social and cultural world of his time, not beyond it. But Hegel thought that we could absorb and live fully, rationally, comprehending, through ideas the world we live in. As we've looked at before, Hegel by the 1820s actually believed that the world in which we found ourselves (and for him, that was Prussia) incorporated the completion of history, if by history you mean the unfolding of the ideas that could and do matter to the human spirit. Hegel, as we know, understood knowledge as a continuing recapitulation and reintegrating, absorbing and appropriating of what already can be and is known in the richness of its full content, but for Hegel, for the tradition, the world, it is revealed that way. Those features can and must be pervasively and constantly the object of rational comprehension.

Let us pause for just a moment. There's a famous remark that Marx makes and it's helpful to note it. Marx says what we need to do is not understand the world. He actually thought that in important ways the world was already understood. Marx thought that the basic problem was to change the world because who we are is dependent on how life in the world is for us, and if we're to believe Marx, we understood all too well what our life in the world is like, and if that should really matter to us, the way our life in the world was for us is not good. Philosophy told us what that world is like, but Marx said the business is not just to understand the world, it's to change it. We must change it and philosophy can't bring that about. So the meaning of life is not going to found through philosophical knowledge, it's going to be found through a kind of acting that changes the world.

Well, Marx understands our most crucial and our most revelatory relation to the world to be through work. The word often used is "labor". We don't really have an adequate term that explains to us exactly what Marx had in mind. I think we understand it easily from our ordinary experience. If the grand philosophical tradition thought that thought was the most important thing, and that that was what mattered, Marx thinks that our concrete practical engagement in the world expresses most fundamentally our own natures as human beings, because our true natures as human beings is not to be thinkers, it is to be agents unavoidably and deeply constitutively involved in productive activities, work activities that are often and importantly cooperative, and that such work activities are not the lower part of our nature, the higher part being what matters, and that would be thought. No, the engagement through the activity of work that we call labor is something that reveals us as we really are, and what it reveals as well is a very malleable world of socioeconomic relations and forces and the natural world through the work we do is drawn into that. The materials of the world become part of that. What Marx tells us is that ideas, the fancy things that philosophers bounce around, they actually are derivative from this matrix of relations and forces.

We should consider this for a moment. We should pause. We should think about what Marx has told us because it represents and extraordinary change in philosophical thinking. We are now told that our actual, and let's even use this word, our ordinary life in the world, our life as workers, hopefully as productive agents involved in work activities, that's where we find the real world. Those activities in that real world, those are the activities that are and reveal to us what our nature is. We're not minds and bodies and our minds think. We are bodily beings who work, and the kind of work that we do and the situations in which we undertake that work, those are what make us who we are, what we are; and if philosophy, as Marx thought, could do little, if anything, about that, then maybe some other kind of activity would be necessary—some other kind of activity that would do something about the world in which we work, if that world is a world that is not just discomforting, but alienating—if it is a world that does not recognize and acknowledge and allow us the full and free expression and the working out the talents of our abilities.

Let's consider further. Marx has a diagnosis, a diagnostic understanding of this alienation we have. The alienation in which the world in which we live isn't supportive of, doesn't nurture our abilities and talents. Understanding our alienation involves at least three sorts of circumstances in which a separation occurs. We are in a way disengaged or alienated from ourselves and we are not in touch with our true underlying nature. He talks about this in a very engaging way. In the positive non-alienated circumstance, where we are working in the world, the "something," the product, that results from our activities—we have productive activities and product comes from them—Marx thinks that in the best circumstance, that product should be made in the way we would choose to make it and the product, when completed, should be ours, and we should be entitled to dispose of it in the manner in which we choose. If this occurs, then we have used our talents as we would wish and we have been involved productively as free and self-determining beings. Marx says if we were to live in that world—Marx thought in his time, we didn't—the result, the product we would make in our own way, on our own terms could then be construed as an expression of our talent, an expression of ourselves as producers, it could be viewed not just as a product but as a dimension of ourselves. It could be construed as part of the very matrix of our nature.

Now, the activities that are involved and results of these activities—the products that we do, that we bring about in our work—are understood by Marx to enter into the very constitution of us as people who are their producers. Through such activities, people, Marx believes, have the opportunity to become who they really are, much more so than through the ideas and thoughts that people might happen to have. Marx, and this itself is revolutionary, construes ideas and thoughts as mere epiphenomena, that is to say, impotent results of underlying activities, but not contributors to these activities—in other words, only effects, not causes. If Hegel and philosophers thought that ideas moved the world, Marx actually thought that the world in which we are enmeshed as employees, as workers, that is the real world and that is the world that determines ideas. It is not ideas that move the world for Marx, it is the actual world from which we find ourselves engaged in work that produce us, whether we are willing to see it or admit it, the ideas that we live by.

Marx not only believes that work is central and that the products we produce are so important that we must be able to produce them in our own way. Marx also thinks that for us to be truly liberated, if we are to be our true selves, and if our talents are to be realized, our time must be our own. That is to say, everyone's time must be subject to the timing and partitioning of time that one chooses. One's time must belong to us. We must not belong to time.

Even as early as the Stoics, and probably before that, we have the notion that our relation to our own time is most intimate, and to give it over to someone else is to impoverish ourselves. There are really two essential questions that we should ask regarding time and they're important to focus on. Does the time in which we live belong to us or does it belong to someone else? Does the time belong to us, or do we belong to it? There is an important experiential distinction between clock and "existential" time. We live by the clock. Sometimes we are altogether tyrannized by the clock. Then we belong to time external to us. But there's another sense of time that's existential time. We don't pay attention to the clock. We have time belonging to us.

I'd like to pause for a moment to tell you an important story that arises out of a Greek philosopher, Seneca, viewed as a Stoic. Seneca makes a remarkable statement. He says there are all kinds of possessions that we have that we would not think of giving over to anyone else, but what's most precious to us is our time and we're giving our time to other people all the time. Isn't that an extraordinary oddity to think things not quite so intimately connected with us as objects we might have? Those we don't give away. But what is most intimately part of us, our time, we tend to be generous with. Seneca thought that was a great problematic paradox in human life.

But now think about it. Marx says that our talents are to be expressed if they are to be realized. We must live in a world not only where it is in the way we choose that the products we produce are produced, but Marx says we must live in a world in which the time in which we do what we do is our time. It is not given over by us or sold by us to someone else. But of course, Marx, we know, is a critic of capitalism, and the capitalism that Marx chose to see was a capitalism in which we are tyrannized by those with the money to pay, who employ us, and those of us who work are employed, and with the money given us, and in return for that money, sell our time to someone else. Marx thought that the world in which he lived in England in the 19th century, was an exploitative world—a world in which capitalists who turned out in his view to be the "bad guys," dominate human beings, paying for their time and therefore at least metaphorically slaving people who must slave their time, must sell the way they do things to those that pay them. And if you sell your time, if you sell the way you do things and give over the products of what you do to the one who employs and pays you, then, supposedly, that person tells you what to do, how to do it, when to do it. That leaves aside what your talents might be and the possibility that maybe the real meaning of life is finding a way to express and use those talents as you choose in your own time and in your own way. Could the meaning of life be finding a way to live in the world in which that was possible? Is that realistic? Well, whether it's realistic or not, for Marx the meaning of life would be to live in a world where you would express your talents as you wished, produced as you wished and your time would be your own. To the extent that didn't occur, you would live in an alienated condition.

Now in the positive condition, the non-alienated circumstance that Marx extols, not only is what you produce yours to produce as you wish and your time your own, the relations that human beings sustain with each other are concrete existential relations that are fully human and involve a wide range of aspects. Think of it this way. Marx thought that in a society where money was what altogether mattered, relations were primarily between buyer, seller, producer, consumer and there's a whole network of capitalistic arrangements that determine who does what and when. The underlying human meaning of these things gets lost. Production becomes everything. Consumption becomes everything. In order to enable it to make it work efficiently, what you've got to do then is mass production. You've got to have lots of money to hire lots of people who will do things as you tell them, as they must be done. Marx thinks in such a world, not only do we get distracted from who we are, also we get alienated from what our underlying talents might be. Almost in passing, Marx says that not the least of the human relations that are sustained is between man and woman. Even as early as the 19th century, he worries that these relations might be subject to economic determinations.

Marx reacts critically to a matrix of relations that sort out primarily economic terms. He is very concerned, as I just mentioned, that if we live in a world where there is buyer or seller, economic competitor, producer and consumer, employer and employee—if that is the primary way in which we are taken up into life—well, then we are not living a concrete human life, and a concrete human life is what ultimately matters. So what then does Marx tell us diagnostically?

Let's consider what he does tell us diagnostically and go further. He tells us that when all is said and done, ideas are the results of circumstances, not the creator of circumstances. Marx tells us that what we think is determined by the kind of life we live in a world we work and that the ideas we have are a result of work arrangements. Marx tells us that if those arrangements do not speak to our talents, do not give us the freedom to develop as we wish, allow us to produce as we wish and allow our time to be our own, that that world in which we then find ourselves must be changed. Philosophy won't be able to change it. Something else will be required to change that world and perhaps what might be required is a radical, revolutionary alteration of that world. Why does Marx think that's needed? Because maybe only then our true talents can be expressed, and if the meaning of life is how we are in the ordinary world as workers, then probably we'll have to look aside from philosophy. We'll have to look at how the world is structured, and what probably we will need to do is to undertake activities that will radically change it.

Where do we find the meaning of life? Not in ideas. Not in withdrawing from the world. For Marx, we find the meaning of life through the radical change in the world that supposedly would liberate our general talents. Is this an unrealistic dream? Is this a misunderstanding of what human life is actually like? Is this a dream that has no future? Is this a dream that's not realistic? Or does Marx tell us something about what the true meaning of life could be if the world was arranged in a different way?

In our next lecture, we'll look into these questions about Marx and about the direction Marx takes.

Lecture Eleven
Marx's Utopian Hope

Scope:

Philosophical strategies for dealing with the world sort out into three types, involving transcendence, resignation, and transformation. Marx believes that we belong to history and that we will find the meaning of our lives through it. The history that he outlines involves oppressive class distinctions, socioeconomic conflict, and the domination of the weaker by the stronger. It is not ideas but property and power—and the forces controlling them—that have moved human history. Marx believes that ideas, taken alone, are not efficacious. Ideas are understood by Marx to be "ideological." They are distortedly employed as a means of deceiving us. Through ideology, our circumstances are represented to us differently than they are, thus anaesthetizing us to our true human condition. Marx is among the first philosophers whose guide to living involves a critique of religion as destructively ideological. He forwards communism as a means of overcoming our alienation and transforming our spirit. For this to happen, however, Marx claims that revolution is necessary. Philosophy itself will not help.

Outline

I. The axial notion that we are *in* but not *of* the world suggests three possible strategies with respect to our relation to the world: transcendence, resignation, and transformation.

    A. The notion of transcendence has played the primary role because of the Greek preference for theory over practice.

        1. The very configuration of the human soul in Plato encourages this consequence.

        2. The Christian notion of a kingdom not of this world has a similar consequence but puts philosophy in the service of considerations of faith.

            a. This development was a watershed, for it made philosophy, construed as an autonomous quest for transcendence, a supporter of religion.

            b. Marx believes, however, that religion is an opiate for the people.

    c. A further and typical consequence has been to transform the use of philosophy as a guide to transcendence into a somewhat secret and/or esoteric pursuit, but Marx dismisses this notion.

    d. One of the consequences of the Enlightenment was the submergence of otherworldliness and the emergence of philosophy out from under the control of theological concerns.

3. As the world came increasingly to be understood scientifically and axial instincts decreased, transcendence came to be understood as escaping the material world and entering into the realm of contemplative thought.

B. Resignation has also been a dominant strategy, almost to the point of being identified with philosophy itself, as in "being philosophical" about things.

    1. Even in Socrates, but especially in Stoic and Hellenistic thought, it is believed that no harm can come to a good person and thus that goodness is a matter of character, something inward. Marx, however, considers this notion to be escapism.

    2. Deontological ethical systems, emphasizing the evaluation of motive over consequence, are frequently sophisticated forms of resignation from the world. Marx disagrees, believing that people can use this notion to dominate others.

    3. Schopenhauer's is also a philosophy of resignation, if not renunciation.

        a. In important ways, Schopenhauer rejects reality itself and might be called "nihilistic."

        b. Marx says that we must accept and change *this* world.

    4. The strategy of resignation lives off an unstable mixture of beliefs regarding the compensatory features of the inner life, the actual insignificance of the world, and what Marx construes as a futile celebration of the world's fruits. Marx views these fruits as unjustly available only to a privileged few.

C. Marx's notion of a philosophical guidance for living, one leading to the world's transformation, has involved the underlying beliefs that worldly life is not just clothing for the human spirit, but essential to it, and that human history is a narrative of progress toward an intended goal, whether that goal is fully and consciously comprehended or not.

  1. Hegel believes that there is a worldly and qualitatively measurable development of the human spirit through history.

   a. Past stages are taken up into the present in reconfigured form.

   b. Ideas matter and, in fact, drive history.

   c. On Hegel's account, the end of history, its goal, has been reached.

  2. Marx focuses on historical development and is famously said to have inverted Hegel.

   a. For Marx, history has not reached its final stage, but that stage can be prospectively predicted and in some ways hastened or at least anticipated.

   b. The complex of socioeconomic forces and their dynamic development configure and define human life. For Marx, ideas are derivative.

   c. The current (and penultimate) stage of development, which Marx refers to as capitalism, involves significant traceable and comprehensible distortions of human life and human consciousness.

   d. As guidance for living, philosophy in Marx transforms into social critique and visionary prophecy.

II. On the Marxist account, socioeconomic forces are sorted out in a capitalist society in terms of ownership and labor. Societal and property configurations within this disposition of resources are said to distort human life and even to make the comprehension of these distortions challenging.

A. This set of historical circumstances is greatly influenced by Hegel's famous "Master and Slave" section of his *Phenomenology of Spirit*.

1. Hegel takes to be fundamental the notion that domination and subordination provide the dynamic that structures human relations.
2. Out of this notion later comes "the politics of recognition."

B. On Marx's account, the dynamic of Master and Slave plays out in capitalism.

1. These laws are said to engender and reinforce alienation.
2. The mode of thinking involved in these circumstances is termed *ideological,* and is said to nurture "false consciousness."
3. For Marx, philosophical guidance involves diagnosis: the detecting and exposure of ideology (claims that give us skewed views of the world) and the dispersal and extinguishing of false consciousness.
4. Rather than being objective, revelatory, and/or transformative, ideology masks the interests of the dominant class and presents these interests as if they were reliable accounts of how the world is and in fact ought to be.
5. Marx decries religion as a particularly effective means of distortion, a means of displacing human energy.
6. Marx gets construed by some as a prophet of social justice.

III. Marx believes that people would revolt and create a communist society, where each person would be rewarded according to his needs and work according to his talents.

Essential Reading:

Karl Marx, *The Marx-Engels Reader.*

Robert Tucker, *Philosophy and Myth in Karl Marx.*

Supplementary Reading:

Ernst Fischer, *The Necessity of Art: A Marxist Approach.*

Questions to Consider:

1. Why is ideology such an important concept in Marx?

2. What is Marx's critique of religion?

3. How does Marx understand our future historical development?

Lecture Eleven—Transcript
Marx's Utopian Hope

Many people have said that we've lived at least 2,000 years and maybe longer with the notion that we don't really belong in this world. We find ourselves in this world, but this isn't the place of our true belonging. Now of course, many have taken that very literally. They have taken it as the notion that we are on a pilgrimage through this life and the end of that pilgrimage is to have reached—of course as some have called it—the Kingdom of Heaven. Others call it "eternity", the notion of a higher realm. Many have talked about the journey of life in that way. Others, however, have thought that can only be a metaphorical notion. There's no "other world" that we can actually attain; no such place exists. But the notion that our true belonging is "elsewhere" is an important metaphor, a metaphor that helps us not get too entrenched in the everyday, ordinary affairs of this life. As we'll see as we go further along, philosophers have argued over whether to understand our having a place of true belonging as a literal notion or a metaphorical notion. They've even been concerned as to whether even as a metaphorical notion it can make sense for us.

Does it make sense to think of life as a journey, and that somehow this world is a place that we have in some way to reorient ourselves in to find a way, at least metaphorically, to transcend? These become pressing issues. Well, as we've seen matters so far, the grand vision hailed with qualifications, but when we came to Schopenhauer, and as we've now come to look at Karl Marx, that vision of our belonging to some "beyond," whether literal or metaphorical, is now brought into deep question. It's as if we primarily are in this world, and in Marx's case, it's really where we belong and we've got to change this world here to make it a world in which we can experience fully that "belonging."

Let's continue now on this strange adventure that we're engaged in. This axial notion—that we are *in*, but not altogether *of* the world—obviously suggests three possible strategies with respect to our relation to the world—transcending it, being resigned to it, or maybe transforming it—and maybe that transformation would be the important thing whether revolutionary or through gradual progress. After all, the notion of revolution which we're going to be looking at in Marx isn't the only way in which we might change the world in which we find ourselves; we could do it with gradual improvements. There are numerous ways it could be done, but let's keep in mind as we go forward that the notions we're looking at now in Marx, have next to nothing to do with some alleged other world. They have to do nearly altogether with how we can transform this world into a place where we can be "at home."

Of course the notion of transcendence has played an important, even primary role in our Western history. That's partly because of the Greek preference for theory over practice. The idea that what really is the highest and enhancing thing we can do is theorize and speculate about ideas. What we begin to see strongly in Marx is the idea that its practice, not only that is important and central, but its actual practice—living and working in the world—that is the place that whatever salvation we may have attained would be attained. That salvation isn't a deliverance *from* the world; it's making the world over into a place where we can be complete, where we can be full, where we can have the completion possible to us. The very configuration that the tradition has given us through Plato of the soul encourages the idea of theory, that theory is really is what matters. Speculation—Marx, as we're seeing, tips that upside down and says that theories and ideas arise from the very concrete circumstances in which we are living our lives and are always going to be enmeshed.

Now, Marx is a very great critic of religion and his criticisms are important, but we have to understand first what he's criticizing before we look too much further into the criticisms themselves. There's the Christian notion, for example, that the Kingdom is not of this world, and that's had a consequence, too, of Western thinking. One thing it has done is put philosophy in the service of considerations of faith. That became a kind of watershed moment in Western philosophy. Hegel, in fact, for all of his talk said that he was a "religious philosopher" and what he was doing was using philosophical ideas to illustrate and articulate the real meaning for sophisticated, educated people of what faith was. Hegel was in a way using philosophy to support religion.

But let us be very clear about this. Hegel might have said that. There might have been the view that philosophy, as said in a certain way, would be a sophisticated, subtle, deep religion for educated people, but as you can imagine, there's another account that emerges, and that account is that philosophy is quite separate from religion. It can be utopian. It can give us a grand picture of another realm, maybe not a literal realm after death, but a realm of ideas or forms or realities that only the philosophical mind can reach, that's something we can consider as possible. What's important to see in Marx is that Marx thinks that doesn't add up. One of Marx's rather strong notions is that religion, as we've known it, is an opium for the people. It is something that should give them to get their minds off the fact that they are being exploited. What Marx says, in effect, is that you can abuse, you can exploit, you can suck the very everyday meaning, talent, expression of talent, life out of people, and they're likely to take it if you tell them that the things of this world don't matter anyway. The best things in life are free, after all. God loves you and "blessed are the meek," because "they inherit the earth," and don't worry that nothing is coming to you now, because the poor are the loved ones and the cherished ones in heaven.

If religion isn't literally true, it is possible that there's a philosophical religion. It's also possible that Marx is onto something, and that's something we have to think about. Does Marx promise us a world that can really be changed here and now? Nobody's going to tell us how to bring it about and hope that it will work out, but Marx does tell us not, absolutely not, to take seriously the claims of religion. If those claims say we're going to be looking toward another world, and if philosophy says, think primarily about ideas, Marx is going to say, "Don't take that too seriously, either." Now, a further consequence of making philosophy as a guide to transcendence is that philosophy can then become cultish and it can become, in effect, an esoteric pursuit. It can be a way of getting away from the serious life we live in the world. Marx dismisses that as well.

One of the consequences of the Enlightenment did turn out to be the submerging of otherworldliness and the emergence of philosophy out from under the control of theological concerns. Marx very much saw that. He was an antagonist toward religion but he was also antagonistic toward philosophy if it was just free from religion, but free simply to spin out ideas. Even in the 19th century with Marx, as the world came increasingly to be understood scientifically, axial instincts—ideas that we could transcend the world, we could find a beyond—decreased because of scientific progress and the very notion of transcending the world got changed into the notion that what you would really do then was simply live a life of the mind, of ideas; an artistic and aesthetic life.

Well, if not transcendence, what about resignation? Resignation has been a strategy to deal with the human predicament, the human situation. It's been a dominant strategy and some people have identified it with philosophy itself, as in "being philosophical" about things. Even in Socrates, Hellenistic thought believed that no harm came to a good person and, thus, that goodness is a matter of character. Resign yourself to what happens in the world. What happens in the world is of no great importance. Resignation is just to accept the world and cultivate the inner life. Marx says that, too, is escapism. It's cowardice. It's an inability to understand that if you resign yourself to the way things are, then the one life you might have had, you won't ever be able to have because resignation is a retreat. Resignation is a kind of amputation of underlying human possibility.

Deontological ethical systems have themselves also been resignation motives. We looked at one in Kant emphasizing motive, not consequence, on such views. You have pure motives, you do what you want to do and then things are as they will be. Whatever the consequences, you can live with those consequences. If you do the right thing, if your motives are right, what happens happens. Marx says no, this idea of purity of motive can also be used by the dominant and ruling people just as much as the notion of another world or philosophy as living in the world of thought and ideas. The notion that you have a pure heart and pure motives could be equally problematic and equally amputate real human possibilities that you have. Well, we've looked at that notion of renunciation in Schopenhauer. The idea that life is a disease and the cure is to be resigned and renounced and not live with the difficult pleasures, pains that it has. We know that Schopenhauer rejects reality and in that sense he is kind of "nihilistic". What Marx tells us is that we have to accept to change to live fully in the world and make the changes in that world that are necessary. Not like Schopenhauer, resigned from the world because life is a disease, no, living fully in the world, and if the world does not meet up with what our human needs are that are social, that are productive, then we take what risks we have to take to alter and change that world. No deep pessimism.

The strategy of resignation lives off an unstable mixture of beliefs regarding that the inner life can compensate for a bad world, that the actual world isn't significant. Marx thinks that's a futile attitude. We ought to be celebrating the fruits of the world. What we ought to do is change the world so that those fruits, those opportunities are not unjustly available to just a privileged few people.

What we need to look closely at is philosophical guidance for living if it involves transcending the world. The meaning of life, Marx thinks, is found in the world itself and if we do not have access to opportunities in that world to develop a meaningful life, then we will have to transform the world. We will have to make it into a different world because after all, our worldly life isn't just external clothing that we wear, we just don't happen to be living in the world. We've got to make that world a home for ourselves. It gives us opportunities to express our talents, express who we are, and we have to view human history as potentially aggressive that it can reach a goal. That the world as we know it—if we confront directly the problems about it that repress us and suppress us—that world can thereby be transformed. Marx picks up so many of these ideas from Hegel. Hegel thinks, as we know, spirit is developed in stages through history and Hegel thinks that the past stages are ones that have been taken up into a present we can celebrate. Hegel has said ideas matter, they drive history and that history is now complete. But Marx speaks differently.

Marx, if we can continue further in following through on his insight or his claim, his mistake is that he focuses on historical development in a way that is commonly said to turn Hegel upside down. Marx says that history hasn't reached its final stage. He says that we can predict what that stage will be and if the meaning of our life is in the world, we can even say something about what the world will have to be life for that stage to be reached. Again, Marx thinks it can be predicted and he thinks that there is a complex of socioeconomic forces that are dynamically developed in the world in which we find ourselves. These configure our lives, ideas that we might reflect on, have "spectatorial" thought on, or are merely derivative. Marx thinks that the current stage of the world in which we find ourselves is the penultimate stage of human development. As we saw in the last lecture, he calls it capitalism, and he thinks that it involves comprehensible, traceable distortions of human life, distortions of human consciousness. Keep in mind, it is Marx's view that how your mind thinks, how you see the world, is a result, a consequence—not a cause of—how the world is. Marx thinks that how the world is, that's the cause of the ideas you have and the way in which you think about the world. So if the meaning of life is to be found through the fulfillment of individuals, and that fulfillment must happen in this world, then we have to look at ways in which this world can and must be changed. Marx thinks he has an account of how this world can and must be changed. Marx in this sense could be called a critic of society who offers a social critique and also a visionary prophet.

Saint Augustine, many centuries ago, had the notion of a "City of God," where people who are true believers could, in a utopian way over time and history—however sinful they were—eventually achieve the result of transformation and salvation. There is an Enlightenment ideal that was in the 18th century. That ideal was that we would use reason and rationally we would gradually change the world. Perhaps in the notion of globalization today, that same rational utopian hope is to be found. Marx thinks that what we need to do is we need to overcome hunger and poverty. We cannot do this through religion. We can't do it through simply a set of ideas. We have to do it through looking in a cold, hard way at what opportunities the world offers and we also have to look at how these opportunities are distributed.

Marx gives us an account of capitalist society in terms of laws of capitalist commodity production. He thinks that we live our lives in terms of ownership and labor. That there are various property configurations and resources are disposed in such a way that there are the "haves" but also the "have-nots," and the world distributes in such a way that the "haves" have an opportunity if they take it, and typically they do, to express their talents when and how they want, and that the "have-nots" do not have these opportunities. They are given ideas or religion, various forms of consolation, but they are not given access to the world in which as human beings, they must have access to the world if they are truly to become fully human and life can be meaningful for them.

This set of historical circumstances—the capital sense that Marx thought existed in his time—he thinks very much is the way things now are, and in his mind it's very influenced by something he finds in Hegel, the early Hegel that he loves. It's in a very famous section of Hegel's *Phenomenology* called "Master and Slave." Hegel says that, in our lives we are always in situations involving dominance and subordination; that, at least metaphorically, there's always a kind of struggle for who will be the dominant one and who will be the subordinate one. Out of that, by the way, we get the "politics of recognition" in our time, where we're always concerned with recognition and who is the dominant recognizer, and who is the subordinate one. Now Hegel takes that and makes that fundamental to human life. Marx takes it and Marx says that it actually plays out in a very, very socio-cultural way that plays itself out in terms of owners, workers, employers and employees, "haves" and "have-nots," and it works out in such a way that some are favored but most are not.

Let us take a moment and think about this. If Marx's account is correct, here's the way it works. Remember now, Marx writes from the 19th century, living in England. Marx says that in the capitalist world, more and more wealth accumulates in fewer and fewer hands. Fewer and fewer people have more and more resources. More and more people have less, and it is Marx's claim that there is a dynamic to the way capitalism works that makes that situation go to an extreme. If it goes to an extreme, what happens is that, with more and more people disenfranchised, having no benefit from the system, deriving nothing from it, being told what to do but not having their talents expressed, revolutionary fervor proceeds. Let's look at this revolutionary fervor further.

Does alienation really occur in circumstances where there is an accumulation of wealth in one place and more and more people do not have opportunity? Well, the motive thinking, Marx thinks, involved in the circumstances takes on what he calls an "ideological caste." What he claims is that in these circumstances, the people on top are always going to find a way tell a story that's going to make it look like this unfair distribution is okay. They can say things like, "the best things in life are free. Don't you worry. What really matters doesn't depend on your socioeconomic circumstances in life," and Marx's claim is that in that capitalist world, a "false consciousness" is developed. We are seduced into thinking that, "well, the fact is, we are either exploited or not, yet an opportunity doesn't matter."

For Marx, philosophical guidance, if we are going to move toward a meaning for our lives, involves diagnosis. We've got to detect and expose ideology; that is, claims that give us a skewed view of the world that make us think that situations which are actually, in some ways, intolerable for us, they're livable because those situations aren't where the locus of meaning is found. Marx always wants to diagnose and look at claims about how things are that might make us quiet and passive that will give us a false consciousness in the world we live in, that doesn't matter as much. Marx is telling us it must matter because it's the only place we can live, it's the only place any meaning can be found.

Rather than being objectively, revelatory, or transformative, Marx claims that ideology really masks the interest of the dominant class and presents those interests as reliable accounts of how the world ought to be. Again, Marx thinks that religion is a particularly effective means of distortion, and as I've said earlier, he refers to it as the "opiate of the masses." It's a means of crowd control, it's a means of displacing human energy, because if your concentration is elsewhere, you may not reach and accept the fact that you are at a certain stage of desperation which can only be overcome if important activity is undertaken to change the world.

I've said little about this as I move now to the end of these remarks on Marx. Marx tells us that revolution is required. He tells us it can be predicted because it's in the nature of the unfair distributions in a capitalist society, that more and more people are disenfranchised, and this disenfranchisement reaches them to the point where, in utter desperation, having nothing to lose, they will completely revolt. Out of that, Marx thinks, will come what is called a communist society. In that society, each person will be rewarded in accordance to the needs that person has and each person will work and act in accordance with the talents that person has. After the revolution, which is a consequence of circumstances becoming intolerable, when more and more people having less and less, having no stake in the system, jump up finally and revolt, on the other side of that—which by the way, critics of Marx have often called "a pie in the sky, by and by"—supposedly we will be liberated to express our true abilities and we will be rewarded in terms of our actual needs.

Well, difficult situation at best, difficult because it didn't happen. That is to say, the revolution didn't come as Marx might have thought it would, and we should mention as a result of its not coming, someone we know a great deal about in the 20th century, Vladimir Lenin, who became for a while of course the leader of Russia—which became the Soviet Union—said these exploited people who aren't finding the meaning of their lives in the world, well, they're not revolting either! So, in Lenin's view there needed to be some vanguard who would lead them and that vanguard, Lenin thought, would be the Communist Party—a political party would provide the leadership and the ideas. In passing, note that Stalin thought that this was a great idea, and especially so for Russia. Stalin wasn't the internationalist. Lenin was the internationalist. But a vanguard, in any case, was needed, and it would be a political party.

Next, let us look no longer in the world in its socio-political circumstances. Let us look at the Self and its inner dimensions. Let us look at the meaning of life as seen through the ideas, the reflections, of Kierkegaard.

Lecture Twelve
Kierkegaard's Crises

Scope:

Large and pervasive phenomena preoccupy the reflections of Hegel, Schopenhauer, and Marx. Philosophical guidance is worked out against the backdrop of history and other impersonal or supra-personal forces. In Danish philosopher Søren Kierkegaard (1813–1855), often labeled the "father of Existentialism," these large-scale considerations fall away. An intense focus is placed upon the individual. A consideration of three crises in Kierkegaard's own life illumines very basic tenets of Existential philosophy itself: the focus on individuality as an accomplishment, not a given, and an extreme concentration on the separateness and inner seclusion required for an authentic and genuinely meaningful human life. Kierkegaard makes the extraordinary claim that a set of three stages must be traversed for a human life to be complete. A consideration of Kierkegaard's own crises allow us to focus the dynamics and message of a religiously oriented Existentialist guide to living.

Outline

I. Before Kierkegaard, the notion of detaching from one's specific individuality and coming to relate (and even belong) to something larger than oneself had dominated much philosophical thinking regarding the best way of living.

   A. The most fundamental means for accomplishing this transcendence was thought to be through the deployment of detached or passionate reason.

      1. Typically, this thought suggested the separability of a higher and a lower aspect of our human nature; the one dispensable, the other essential.

         a. Assuming that only *like* could know *like*—and that truth was eternal—it was possible to conceive a part of oneself as being immortal. This rational capacity achieved a special dignity for some philosophers.

         b. At a minimum, a kind of "objective" immortality was suggested: direct knowledge of what does endure, whatever happens to oneself.

2. Great struggles may nonetheless be involved in the subduing of our lower nature, if our higher nature is to have its full opportunity to develop.

    a. In Augustine, one's sensual nature is a great stumbling block, as it is for many of the Stoics.

    b. We have seen that the passions were believed to be directed toward the transitory and unimportant.

B. The form that the quest for transcendence took in Kierkegaard's time was *historical*. The comprehension of the blueprint of history itself was sought. It did not matter whether one actually contributed personally to historical developments or not.

    1. Danish Hegelians, for example, were contributors to the dialectical development of various aspects of Danish history.

    2. Kierkegaard detests this spectatorial detachment. He extols the passionate and committed *living through* of various events.

    3. Kierkegaard wants to make life more difficult.

    4. He understands the active *"living through"* of something to be very specific, concrete, and individual and as having no particular "rationality" in terms of an explicable, repeatable pattern.

II. Part of Kierkegaard's "Existentialism" is captured in the very specific circumstances he details in his *Fear and Trembling,* regarding the Biblical story of Abraham and Isaac.

A. Kierkegaard construes Abraham's willingness to sacrifice his son, Isaac, as a "teleological suspension of the ethical."

    1. Morally, it is utterly wrong that Abraham should slay his son, and it remains morally wrong.

    2. That Abraham is commanded by God to perform this sacrifice does not make it morally right, but makes it something Abraham must do. Such a command from God is in fact the only justification for acting in this manner.

    3. Kierkegaard hopes to undercut all human claims to creativity insofar as they are employed as justifications for disregarding morality.

4. For Kierkegaard, actions such as Abraham's are the essence of defining "crisis" situations in human life. They are neither rational nor transferable beyond the concrete situation out of which they arise.

B. Kierkegaard's own life involves an "Abrahamic" circumstance, and it focuses his religious Existentialism.

    1. Kierkegaard breaks his marriage engagement to Regine Olsen, claiming to spare her in so doing.

    2. Though he claims his melancholy to be a motivating reason, Kierkegaard actually believes that he needs to "sacrifice" Regine for the sake of his God-relationship. He believes that this God-relationship must not be diluted.

        a. Wholehearted, singleminded, and undistracted commitment to God—a leap of faith—is Kierkegaard's conception of the only complete life.

        b. Kierkegaard seeks purity of heart.

        c. Such a life is inward and largely hidden.

    3. Kierkegaard distinguishes between a "knight of faith" and a "knight of resignation."

        a. Kierkegaard believes that knights of resignation, who display their religion, their poverty, and their humility, and who resign from the ordinary pleasures of life, are really calling attention to themselves.

        b. The faith of the knights of faith, on the other hand, is inward, hidden, and personal.

C. Another crisis in Kierkegaard's life illustrates his notion of our underlying, if almost always uncomprehended, separateness and isolation from others.

    1. Kierkegaard challenges a satirical journal, *The Corsair*, to satirize him, which it does at great social cost to Kierkegaard.

    2. Altogether unlike Hegel, Kierkegaard claims that our relations to others are false reassurances and *ersatz* support systems.

    3. For Kierkegaard, security is a form of death.

III. Kierkegaard's relation to the State Church of Denmark becomes a defining crisis for him upon the death of Bishop Jakob Mynster and a subsequent eulogy delivered by Professor Hans Martensen at Myster's funeral.

A. Kierkegaard claims that only a direct spiritual connection to God, not one mediated by any other individual or by an institution, is desirable and even possible.

    1. Unlike Hegel, Kierkegaard believes institutional settings to falsely hijack, not enhance, the human soul.

    2. Kierkegaard explains true spiritual relatedness to be necessary for salvation. For him, it is attainable by no visible means, and true Christianity is offensive to human reason.

    3. According to Kierkegaard, if you believe in Christianity because it makes sense, you have misunderstood Christianity.

B. On Kierkegaard's account, even to reach the point where a true spiritual commitment can be made, prior stages have to be lived fully and overcome.

    1. Kierkegaard believes individuality is attained only after reflections on oneself.

    2. Unlike secular Existentialism, Kierkegaard believes our true nature to exist and only fully to be reached in a specific relation to God.

C. As a guide to living, Kierkegaard uses philosophy rigorously and intensely to show philosophy's ultimate unimportance and irrelevance in the face of what really matters.

Essential Reading:

Søren Kierkegaard, *Papers and Journals: A Selection.*

Walter Lowrie, *A Short Life of Kierkegaard.*

Supplementary Reading:

Joakim Garff, *Søren Kierkegaard: A Biography.*

Questions to Consider:

1. Which of Kierkegaard's crises seem valid as explanations of his philosophical views?

2. Why does Kierkegaard find our separateness from other people so important?

Lecture Twelve—Transcript
Kierkegaard's Crises

In our journey together, we've looked at some overarching and grand ideas about the meaning of life. If we look back on them, they're fairly complicated and complex. But recently, it's as if maybe, the way these ideas have spun out through philosophy, we've reached a kind of dead end and become dead ended. Now there might be some agonies we have over the meaning of life, but unlike Schopenhauer I don't think life is to us, such a burden that we want simply not to think any longer about its meaning and hope that life doesn't last too long. Even though many of us work nine to five, or maybe from six in the morning until midnight and don't necessarily find the world in which we work one that meets our talents, at the same time I doubt we contemplate revolution. I think our view is that we will find time to pursue questions of meaning, maybe even more so if we have the opportunity to retire. But in any case, we are making a turn now of a significant nature because the overarching pictures that we have seen in our previous lectures, are pictures of a grander world, or even in Marx, "the world at large," that might be changed. With Kierkegaard—and Søren Kierkegaard is a Danish philosopher who lives in the first half of the 19th century—the emphasis is on the individual.

Kierkegaard is what is called an "existentialist," and his concern is to help us see that we must become individuals. We're not simply individuals to begin with. Before Kierkegaard, the notion of detaching from one's specific individuality and coming to relate, and even belong, to something larger than oneself had dominated much philosophical thinking regarding the best way to live. A most fundamental means for accomplishing this kind of transcendence of our ordinary life was thought to be through the deployment of maybe a detached reason or maybe a passionate reason. Typically, what this suggested was that we did have a lower and higher nature and that we could somehow dispense with, or at least make less strong, that lower nature and that that higher nature of ours, our true and essential nature, probably connected with our human reason, could then lift us, and in lifting us, help us find that higher level where meaning could be discovered. Actually, in the Greeks, the idea was, if we could detach and transcend in this way and we did find something that was of lasting value that probably meant that there was something of lasting value in us. What it suggested was that, well, only like can know like and that truth is eternal and we can know it, well, maybe there's something eternal or immortal about us and that our rational capacity to seek this out shows that we have a genuine dignity. At a minimum, even if our life ends with life and we would never be again, there's still the kind of notion of "objective" immortality. Though we die, we can at least have known what matters, that there are things that matter that will always be and we can know them.

Of course, in the history of philosophical thinking there have been great struggles, great struggles that have been involved in the subduing of our lower nature and in developing of our higher nature and giving it a chance to develop. Agonizing concerns in philosophy and religion, through Augustine, the idea of one's sensual nature is a great stumbling block as it was seen to be by many people after Socrates in the Greek world where things are falling apart. We've seen very clearly that the passions were believed to be directed towards the transitory, the unimportant, and we would have to rise above that.

Now the form that the quest for transcendence for our lower nature took in Kierkegaard's time turned out to be quite *historical*. What was sought was a comprehension of some kind of blueprint of history itself. It did not matter whether one actually contributed personally to history or to historical developments but one could at least understand it. Kierkegaard, living in Copenhagen, Denmark, read and reflected on a number of thinkers we call "Danish Hegelians". Unlike Hegel's view of the "vast sweep" of history of the development of the Western spirit, the Danish Hegelians talked about the dialectical development of Denmark and the history of this and the history of that. Kierkegaard thought that was just absurd. These were probably, in the worse sense, academics who had read some Hegel and thought, "Well, Hegel had said all these things that we here in Denmark, we can talk about things too!" Now they didn't do this but it is as if they said, "Let us give the history of the stages of dialectical development of Danish pastry!" Kierkegaard thought they were just into trivialities but very, very pompously so.

So, in a famous passage of Kierkegaard's, he talks about himself. And what he says in this passage is that, well he's sitting at a sidewalk café, and he's thinking about the fact that everybody's making life easier and he's thinking of the Danish Hegelians that make it easier, so to speak, to understand the development of this, the development of that—even as I suggested, but of course I don't fully mean it—Danish pastry. What Kierkegaard says is, "I want to be famous and important too! So what I'm going to do is try to find a way to make things more difficult." He says at that point, the cigar that he was smoking went out and he had to take a moment to light it. He says this because he is going to begin to get us to think that the small, the trivial, the seemingly unimportant, the incidental things in life kind of matter too, and these pompous academic philosophers with these abstract concepts who don't pay full attention to the close, little details of life, well, they're fundamentally missing something that is very important. Because, as human beings such as you, and such as I, all kinds of things enter into our lives and even contribute to the meaning of our lives and we need to pay attention to them. We need to pay a great attention to them.

Kierkegaard thinks that meaning in life is found through "living through" very specific, concrete and individual situations that don't necessarily have any overall "rationality". If we could paraphrase a notion, he says, "The crowds might fill the plaza full but probably there's only one there that knows the truth and that's the one that fights the bull." Kierkegaard has diatribes about the press, which he claims is always throwing out this and that and in throwing out this and that, getting us caught up in conventional ideas, not thinking things through for ourselves and if we're not up with the press, maybe we're reading these fancy history books. Not history of life, but history of dialectical ideas, and for him, that's not where life is going to be found.

Actually, Kierkegaard's "existentialism", as it is called, is captured in some very specific circumstances that he details in a book called *Fear and Trembling*. It's based on the Biblical story of Abraham and Isaac. Kierkegaard tells this story in a very moving way, if philosophers can be moving. Abraham is asked to sacrifice his son, Isaac and he takes his son up to be sacrificed. Kierkegaard talks about this under a concept that he calls the "teleological suspension of the ethical". What does he mean by that? Well it should come as no surprise that there could morally be no justification that you would take the life of your son. That it is absolutely morally wrong to do so and it would not take a great deal of insight to see that. However, Kierkegaard broods on the fact that God has commanded Abraham to make this sacrifice. Here we come to the core point. Kierkegaard says that because God has commanded it, Abraham must do it, but it doesn't, in any sense we can comprehend, make it morally right that it is done. It is justified for a higher reason and that higher reason is precisely that it has been God's command that that be done. When Kierkegaard talks this way, what he's trying to do among other things is undercut an idea we've seen in Hegel—that there's the moral plane of life, and there's the creative plane, and that great people are not always morally good people. But some of the great creators of the world nonetheless do things that are immoral or amoral, and cause suffering for others, but if the creative spirit lives through them and they contribute something further to the human spirit, well so be it and that's fine.

When Kierkegaard talks about Abraham and Isaac, Kierkegaard wants us to think that there could only be one reason to transcend the moral, and that would be a command by God. Now, that's an extreme case, but such a case for Kierkegaard, that case that he dwells on is essential and in its essence it defines a crisis situation for human beings in human life. These crisis situations on his view are neither rational, they're not articulate or communicable in any easy way to other people, but they're very concrete situations and out of them, our lives become what they truly are.

Now this is not just a story about Abraham. This is also, as it turns out, a story about Kierkegaard. As we move forward now in a way that we didn't before, we're going to be looking at the lives of some of these philosophers who are talking to us about the meaning of life. We didn't say much about Kant's life. We didn't say much about Hegel's life. We didn't say much about Schopenhauer or Marx's lives. But to understand Kierkegaard, who is called the "father of existentialism," we have to look a little bit at his life because he thinks that Abraham and Isaac's story, which he tells, that illustrates that only God's command would justify our transcending the realm of the moral, he thinks that there was an exemplification of that in his own personal life.

Now some will think—and it's quite easy to think, I believe, in our time—that not much should be made of this, but we have to keep closely in mind that this is the Kierkegaard of the 1840s in Copenhagen. Kierkegaard breaks an engagement he has with Regine Olson. She's much younger than he, and he claims he's doing it in order to spare her. He's going to be sparing her from something. Her father comes over, virtually begs Kierkegaard to keep the engagement. The girl, Regine, is distraught. Kierkegaard is in anguish over doing this, but he tells Regine, that he, Kierkegaard, has melancholy, and he couldn't subject over a lifetime, in marriage— and marriages really did tend to last until death at this time—he was afraid that the melancholy that would be afflicted on Regine would be too much for her. But he also said in his writings that writing about her was more enjoyable than being with her. But there's a third thing that comes through in his writings. That is, that as Abraham was asked to sacrifice Isaac and that for a special relationship with God. It is as if Kierkegaard believes that Kierkegaard has to sacrifice Regine Olson, in order to have a complete and full relationship with God. Kierkegaard thinks Kierkegaard's relationship with God must not be diluted. And of course, as we know, let's pause and think about this for a moment, it worked out for Abraham, didn't it? Because, after all, there was an alternate sacrifice provided and Abraham, at the last minute, didn't have to sacrifice his son.

However, in Kierkegaard's view and in his own experience, Kierkegaard had to follow through and could not reclaim Regine, could not revoke his breaking of the engagement. He had to give her up. He had to give her up—why? Kierkegaard had come to believe that a whole-hearted, single-minded, undistracted commitment—a leap of faith in which the one and only intimate relationship you have is with God—that that would be the only full life. Only in that intense, personal relationship with God would any meaning of life be found, and that would give one a pure heart, and only by developing a pure heart would that relationship be possible. So if Hegel says we can "spectatorially" re-experience a narrative about history, if Marx says, "Oh, there has to be a revolution so the world we live in meets our needs and allows us to express our talents," if Kant talks about a moral life in which our duty is always fighting against our inclinations, Kierkegaard tells us that the true meaning of our lives is within us and inward largely, if not completely, hidden and no one else can truly know it, touch it, understand it, and that inner life itself only finally makes sense if it is a relationship with God. In this respect, Kierkegaard is a very Christian thinker. Kierkegaard understands himself to be a Christian, and so the relationship that he thinks that has to exist with God is on Christian terms.

He makes a very, very important distinction between, well, what could be called a "knight of faith"—think of someone in armor riding on a horse in the Middle Ages—and another kind of knight. Think of him also with armor and riding on a horse—a "knight of resignation". So we have a knight of faith and a knight of resignation. He has trouble with people who he calls "knights of resignation" because he thinks they call attention to themselves. Let's think of them as those who display their religion. They want you to know they're religious. They may be directly part of very organized religion. They may display their humility, their poverty, and they may even go about in particular garbs. Kierkegaard says those resigned people, who resign themselves from ordinary pleasures in life, what they're really doing is they're calling attention to themselves.

The knight of faith—again we have this person in armor, a medieval warrior, except for Kierkegaard it's somebody in Denmark in the middle of the 19th century—the knight of faith's faith is inward, unseen. You meet this person but you don't know that this is a knight of faith. You don't know that this is a knight of faith at all. You just see someone and you can never read from their external appearances what they are really like. But Kierkegaard's intense claim is that only a religion hidden, only known to you, in which it is all about your personal relationship with God that you don't display to anyone else. It is a way through which you can actually find and be one with the meaning of life.

There's another crisis in Kierkegaard's life, which I think underlies and explains why he thought that separateness and isolation from others was a very essential thing. The relationship that God was to be the primary relationship what Kierkegaard has in relations with others as well, that tells us that we must be sure not to be connected with others in any significant way. We must find opportunities to keep separation. There was a satirical journal in Copenhagen. It was called *The Corsair*. It satirized people but it ignored Kierkegaard. Kierkegaard challenges it to satirize him and finally it does! In a way, this is a sad story because the satire was biting. The satire was cruel. As a consequence there would be pictures of Kierkegaard that appeared in the Danish newspapers with his hunched back—he was a hunchback—walking through Copenhagen, and it's in fact the case that little boys in Copenhagen, recognizing Kierkegaard, would throw stones at him. You see, someone would say, "That's terrible!" Not Kierkegaard. He thought he forced the situation in which even if he wanted connection with others, it was made difficult. That's because when it came down to it, Kierkegaard believed that security, the reassurance you get through life with others, is a kind of death. It is the sort of thing that anesthetizes you. What we do, he thinks, so often is we put on faces to meet the faces that we meet. What we probably have is an inner agony and if we can find the religious it can only be through cultivating in secrecy and in inwardness that agony.

Kierkegaard had a peculiar relation to the Church of Denmark and that became another defining crisis in his life. A bishop in the Church of Denmark died. His name was Jakob Mynster and a eulogy was given for him by a professor named Martensen. Martensen said that Mynster, the bishop, was just another in a long line of witnesses to the truth. Well, Kierkegaard was outraged and started writing articles saying, "Is this the witness? Is this the truth? Is there some long chain? That's a mockery!" Why does he say this? He says this because he thinks you can relate to God. I can relate to God. But there are no linkages that can relate us to God through the historical development of something like a church. It can't be done that way. What he says in some of his writings is a person living at the same time as Jesus—and remember, Hegel thought he was a Christian, Kierkegaard thought he was a Christian—for Kierkegaard, as a Christian, even if you walked next to Jesus and lived then, you were no closer to Jesus than you would be believing in Jesus, for Kierkegaard in the 19th century or for us now. So the notion of historical tradition of the church, Kierkegaard thought was a mockery. Only individuals could know God.

Unlike Hegel, Kierkegaard believes that institutional settings falsely hijack the soul, and they give us a false sense of reassurance. They don't enhance our being, our soul, and the true quest for and discovery of meaning in life, and he has a funny story to tell about this. He says if you really believe in the Church and you really believe the doctrine that you have to be baptized to be saved, well, would you take anybody else's word for it? Wouldn't you go and make sure that it happened? Maybe your parents were confused that day and you weren't actually baptized. To this talk about these beliefs and that, "Oh, we're baptized and now we're part of the Church and we're saved," Kierkegaard said, "Get serious. If you really believe that stuff, would you take it on faith if your mother or father or your guardian said, 'Oh, we took care of those things. We know you have to be baptized to be saved. Don't worry, we did it'." Well, wouldn't you worry if we weren't just talking about whether we got tickets for a baseball game, but rather something was done— baptism, which was necessary for our eternal salvation? Kierkegaard thinks that true spiritual relatedness is necessary for salvation but, for him, it's not attainable by any visible means. In fact—and this is something we need to dwell on—Kierkegaard thinks that Christianity he thinks is the way to the meaning of life; that Christianity he thinks only comes to individuals—you, me, every single individual—that Christianity, which Kierkegaard takes to be true—he says, is offensive to our human reason. Bluntly put, Kierkegaard's claim is that if you think that the reason you believe in Christianity is because it makes sense, you've misunderstood Christianity.

On Kierkegaard's account, even to reach the point where a true, spiritual commitment could be made, you need to go through prior stages. You have to live through, in fact, three of them, and in our next lecture we're going to be talking about those stages that we go through. However, it's important to note that for Kierkegaard, reason must be used to its fullest in order for us to experience that, finally, reason won't get us there, and in fact we must use reason to its fullest in order to discover that where we're going to find the meaning of life, from a rational standpoint, doesn't make sense. Think of the contrast. Hegel has said that history is the development of the spirit. It is the narrative story of God's consciousness and we can give a rational account of that story. Kierkegaard says, "Oh yes, we must use our reason, but we must use our reason only to reflect on ourselves, in our own situation, and we, at the end of the full use of our reason, must experience that our reason finally doesn't work." He's not, in this sense, a mushy irrational. He says that someone can discover that reason won't do the job only after the thorough and complete use of it. But again, that use is in a set of reflections regarding oneself, and the problem is to find a way in the midst of this and this reflection on oneself, to realize that one somehow isn't, but must, become an individual.

Unlike secular existentialism—existentialism having nothing to do with religion—Kierkegaard believes that our true nature—something that has yet to be developed by most people—for it to exist and to be fully reached, there has to be a very specific relationship to God. Now as a guide to living, Kierkegaard does use philosophy. He uses it to mock Hegel, mock the Danish Hegelians and he uses philosophy rigorously to show that that kind of thinking, rational thinking—well, it's fancy, it's intricate—but when it comes down to it, it's not altogether relevant. It doesn't help us as individuals, even before we become religious, in the intensely personal aspects of our lives.

Well, in our next lecture together, we have to look to see how it is that Kierkegaard tells us we can go through stages and arrive at this religious life, which he claims is the true meaning of life.

Timeline

1596 ....Birth of Descartes

1650 ....Death of Descartes

1697 ....Publication of Bayle's *Historical and Critical Dictionary*

1712 ....Birth of Rousseau

1724 ....Birth of Kant

1744 ....Birth of Herder

1749 ....Birth of Goethe

1756 ....Birth of Mozart

1762 ....Birth of Fichte; Publication of Rousseau's *Social Contract*

1769 ....Birth of Napoleon

1770 ....Birth of Hegel and Beethoven

1774 ....Publication of Goethe's *Sorrows of Young Werther*

1776 ....U.S. Declaration of Independence

1778 ....Death of Rousseau

1781 ....Publication of Kant's *Critique of Pure Reason*

1788 ....Birth of Schopenhauer

1789 ....Outbreak of the French Revolution

1791 ....Death of Mozart

1793 ....Publication of Kant's *Religion Within the Bounds of Reason Alone*

1800 ....Publication of Fichte's *Vocation of Man*

1803 ....Death of Herder

1804	Napoleon crowned emperor; death of Kant
1805	Beethoven's *Eroica* Symphony
1806	Birth of John Stuart Mill
1807	Publication of Hegel's *Phenomenology of Spirit*
1808	Publication of Goethe's *Faust, Part I*
1813	Birth of Kierkegaard; birth of Wagner
1814	Death of Fichte
1818	Birth of Marx
1819	Publication of Schopenhauer's *World as Will and Idea*
1820	Birth of Engels
1821	Publication of Hegel's *Philosophy of Right*
1823	Beethoven's *Ninth Symphony*
1827	Death of Beethoven
1831	Death of Hegel
1832	Death of Goethe
1843	Publication of Kierkegaard's *Either/Or* and *Fear and Trembling*
1844	Birth of Nietzsche
1848	Publication of Marx's *Communist Manifesto*
1855	Death of Kierkegaard
1856	Birth of Freud
1859	Birth of Husserl and Dewey; publication of Darwin's *Origin of the Species*

1860	Death of Schopenhauer
1867	Publication of Marx's *Capital* (Part 1, Vol. 1)
1872	Publication of Nietzsche's *Birth of Tragedy*
1873	Death of John Stuart Mill
1882	Première of Wagner's opera *Parsifal*
1883	Death of Marx and Wagner
1886	Publication of Nietzsche's *Beyond Good and Evil*
1887	Publication of Nietzsche's *Toward a Genealogy of Morals*
1889	Nietzsche's collapse into insanity; birth of Heidegger
1895	Death of Engels
1900	Publication of Freud's *Interpretation of Dreams*; death of Nietzsche
1905	Birth of Sartre
1913	Birth of Camus
1914–1918	First World War
1926	Birth of Foucault
1927	Publication of Heidegger's *Being and Time*
1929	Birth of Habermas
1930	Publication of Freud's *Civilization and its Discontent*
1933	Heidegger becomes rector of Freiburg University in Germany

1938 ....Death of Husserl; publication of Sartre's *Nausea* and Freud's *Moses and Monotheism*

1938 ....Freud moves from Vienna to London to escape Nazism

1939 ....Death of Freud

1939–1945 ....Second World War

1942 ....Publication of Camus' *The Stranger*

1943 ....Publication of Sartre's *Being and Nothingness*

1951 ....Publication of Camus' *The Rebel*

1952 ....Death of Dewey

1960 ....Death of Camus

1961 ....Publication of Foucault's *Madness and Civilization*

1976 ....Death of Heidegger; Publication of Foucault's *The History of Sexuality*, Vol. 1: An Introduction

1980 ....Death of Sartre

1984 ....Death of Foucault

1985 ....Publication of Habermas's *The Philosophical Discourse of Modernity*

Glossary

Absolute Spirit (Hegel): The historical unfolding of human consciousness. This is construed by Hegel as the insightful replacement for (and successor to) the traditional notion of God. In its totality, Absolute Spirit is said to be the history that "God" is producing as human life unfolds.

Aestheticism: The doctrine that most principles, and especially moral ones, can be and are derived from personal preferences or temperamental inclinations regarding beauty.

Agnostic: The position of those who doubt that certain questions have attainable answers that will be convincing to them, or that a reliable course of action can be determined through these answers. Often, agnostic people make no attempt to come to a definite conclusion on a particular matter.

Alienation (Marx): Disconnection from or insufficient connection with something to which you belong and that constitutes an essential part of your nature.

Ancient: Going back in history to pre-Christian (Greek and Roman) times.

Angst: A notion found especially in Existential philosophy: the feeling of dread or anxiety arising from an often-suppressed awareness that we cannot escape the human predicament and its pervasive problems.

Antecedent: Something that happened before or existed prior to something else (and may continue to exist).

Anthropological: Relating to the study of human attitudes, practices, and artifacts, especially the study of cultures.

Anthropomorphism: The attribution of human characteristics, form, or behavior to nonhuman and possibly even nonexistent realities, such as deities in mythology.

Antinomy: Two apparently correct and reasonable theses that do not agree, exhaust the available options, cannot hold up to thorough scrutiny, and therefore produce an uncertain and bewildering conclusion.

Apollo (Nietzsche): Greek god, patron of music and poetry, construed as the principle of form, organization, and order.

Aufhebung **(Hegel)**: (German) Technical term in Hegel for the abandoning of a conflicted, perhaps even contradictory, outcome and the carrying forward of its conflicting elements into a seemingly reorganized and harmonious context.

Augustinian: Relating to St. Augustine of Hippo (the 4th–5th-century church father), to his doctrines, or to any of his ideas regarding spiritual life.

Axial: The conduct of life construed as a journey from darkness to light and from bondage to liberation; the underlying assumption that there are two orders: that of *this* world (appearance) and that of *another* (reality).

Being: The most basic and pervasive constituent of reality, without which nothing could exist.

Bifurcate: To split or separate off into two parts.

Bolshevism: The ideology and policies of the most radical communist movement in Russia around the time of the Russian Revolution, especially the advocacy of the forcible overthrow of capitalism in the pursuit of a socialist order and command economy.

Buddhism: The teaching of Gautama Buddha, which proclaims that all human life involves suffering, that sorrows arise from attachments, and that attachment can be eradicated through a disciplined life involving both disengagement and compassion.

Capitalism: An economic system based on private ownership and characterized by the rule of law, transparency in transactions, and a free and competitive market motivated by considerations of profit.

Cartesian: Relating to the 17th-century French philosopher René Descartes, who claimed that mind and matter are separate realities and that we can experience directly only the contents of our own minds.

Consumerism: The belief that buying and selling various items is our basic and most desirable relation to the world and that it can bring happiness.

Contextualize: To place an idea within a particular framework or setting in which it may be seen differently and understood better.

Contractual: Involving an agreement that two or more parties voluntarily enter into and consider binding for all parties involved.

Cyclical history: The theory that there are phases of development that recurrently reach completion and then repeat themselves over and over again in largely the same sequence.

Deontological: Relating to philosophical theories that claim that the moral value of an action depends on its motivation, not on its consequences.

Depth psychology: The study of dimensions of human consciousness that are beneath its surface and typically hidden from view.

Derivative: Arising from and influenced by sources beyond itself and therefore not original.

Despotism: Involving the rule and arbitrary use of power, typically, by an individual who has monopolized power and is not accountable to anyone.

Dialectic: The pursuit of truth through discussions that question assumptions; the intellectual tension that exists when two or more conflicting ideas are brought into relation.

Dionysus (Nietzsche): Greek god of fruitful abundance and wine who was often celebrated in orgies. In Nietzsche, Dionysus represents unbounded and often chaotic and destructive energy.

Empathy: The ability to identify with and understand another person's feelings or difficulties from that particular person's own point of view.

Empirical: Based on direct and usually verifiable observation and experiment rather than speculative theory.

Endemic: Characteristic of or unavoidably present in a particular place, or as part of a particular reality or situation.

Enlightenment: An intellectual movement that began in Western Europe in the 18th century and that continues to be very influential. It emphasizes reason and science in the study of human nature and in the explanation of all aspects of reality.

Entschlossenheit **(Heidegger)**: (German) Resoluteness; an underlying steadfastness in outlook, orientation, and commitment.

Episteme (Foucault): A defining principle employed to sort out and configure human knowledge as well as social arrangements.

Epistemology: The branch of philosophy that focuses on the nature of human knowledge; in particular, its foundations, limitations, scope, reliability, and validity.

Eros: The god of love in ancient Greece. Perhaps best construed, especially in Plato, as an underlying, uncomprehended desire for something that is lacking.

Ersatz: A substitute for something that is the original and presumed to be of superior quality.

Ethical: Consistent with agreed upon (and thus seldom achieved) principles of acceptable moral conduct.

Existentialism: A 19th- and 20th-century philosophical movement that often denies that the universe has an intrinsic meaning or purpose; it urges people to focus upon their own particular lives and to take individual and unapologetic responsibility for their own actions.

Faith: Belief in, devotion to, and/or trust in somebody or something without rational certainty that such commitment is warranted.

Fideism: The view that religious knowledge, when all is said and done, depends upon faith and/or revelation.

Formalism: A strong or excessive emphasis on structure; the outward appearance of something instead of its purported content or meaning.

Forms (Plato): The nature or essence of a thing; that which makes a thing what it is. In Plato, forms are considered to exist apart from the particular items that embody them.

Grace: In Christianity, the infinite favor, mercy, and love shown to humankind by God. Through grace, humans are said to be capable of redemption and salvation.

Hellenistic: Concerned with or characteristic of those ideas embedded in Greek civilization from roughly the 4th century B.C. to the 1st century A.D.

Historicism: The belief that each period of history has its own features, beliefs, and values and can only be understood in its own terms. Typically, the conception of universal and enduring values that transcend historical circumstances is denied.

Human predicament: The human situation construed as involving unavoidable, common, and pervasive problems in need of understanding and (hopefully) some measure of resolution.

Iconoclasm: The frequently disorienting and destructive overturning of traditional, religiously significant customs, beliefs, and values.

Imagination (Kant): A blind but indispensable function of the human soul; a power on a level deeper than reason that is involved in producing images and ideas.

Immunity: Exemption from outside interference in the carrying out of one's activities in a particular realm. Such interference is typically understood to come from either government or nongovernmental agencies or individuals. Government itself is usually construed as the appropriate protector of individuals from such interfering activities.

Imperative: Absolutely necessary or unavoidable.

Impotence of Reason (Schopenhauer): The view that, however insightful, reason is incapable of remedying or resolving the problems it reveals.

Last Man (Nietzsche): A person devoid of all strength and courage. Such a person is inclined merely to consume and is then himself or herself consumed by the trivialities of life *in* this world only.

Meaning: The significance of something, its end-purpose, or the insight it reveals.

Messianic: Relating to an inspirational, often charismatic leader, especially one claiming to be a liberator or savior.

Metaphysical: Relating to the study of that which may be beyond the physical world.

Modernity: In philosophy, the period commencing after the Middle Ages, roughly the turn into the 17th century. Modernity is associated with the rise of science and the gradual abandonment of tradition, custom, and otherworldly concerns.

Moral life: Life lived according to a set of ideas regarding what is right and therefore ought to be done—and what is wrong and therefore ought to be avoided.

Mutuality: A relationship between individuals that involves a reciprocal sharing of concerns and that takes their mutual feelings and perspectives into account.

Narcissism: In psychiatry, a personality disorder characterized by an obsession with and an overestimation of one's own ability and appearance. An excessive need for admiration from others is typically present, indicating—somewhat paradoxically—an underlying sense of little worth or even worthlessness.

Nihilism: The rejection of metaphysical and religious beliefs and an attendant sense that life has no reliable foundation or meaning.

Noumenal: Pertaining to that which is beyond the empirical world (that which is based on direct observation) and can only be known or identified, and potentially encountered, by the intellect or reason, not by the senses.

Objectification: To construe or to perceive something, in some cases misleadingly, as a thing, an object.

Objective (Hegel): The philosophical belief that moral truths and external objects and ideas generally exist independently of specific individual minds and perceptions.

Objective Right (Hegel): That to which you are entitled and that complements and completes your nature as a rational being.

Ocular: Perceived or having access to by means of the eye; features so revealed are said to be ocular.

Omnipresent: Continuously and simultaneously present throughout the whole of reality; present all the time and everywhere.

Ontological: Concern with the nature of things and their underlying being. Some claim that no such reality exists beyond what science can determine and thus that nothing is ontological.

Oracularism (Heidegger): To be prophetic in a somewhat mysterious and unaccountable way.

Paradigmatic: That which sets the standard and implies rules for evaluation and further investigation in a particular domain.

Paradox: A statement or proposition that goes contrary to our normal intuitions and appears surprising and often even false or absurd.

Paralogism (Kant): In logic, an invalid argument that has gone unnoticed. It involves conclusions that the premises of an argument may appear to support but, upon closer analysis, do not justify.

Perennial: Constantly recurring; sometimes construed simply as lasting for an indefinite time.

Phenomenology: The science or study of things as they are *perceived* rather than as they may actually *be* apart from their appearance to us; the philosophical investigation and description of our conscious experience without reference to whether what is experienced has independent reality.

Platonic: Relating to the ideas and philosophy of Plato. Plato believed reality to be eternal and unchanging and available to us by means of our reason.

Postmodern: The view that there is no credible narrative that explains our human history and its likely future. The view that there is no foundation upon which our experience rests that could secure its meaning.

Radical: Related to the basic nature or most important features of something in an extreme way.

Realism: The theory that things exist independently of our thoughts and perceptions and can be directly known to us. Sometimes construed as the acceptance of things as they are, as opposed to how we might want them to be.

Reality: How things really *are*, as opposed to an idealized, imaginary, or false way in which they may appear to us. Often contrasted with appearance or illusion.

Reason: Understood by the Greeks as the unique feature of humans, reason is sometimes identified with thought.

Reflexivity: The relation that something has to itself. People, for example, are said to have a certain conception of themselves and thus possess self-relatedness (reflexivity).

Representationalism: The theory that the mind has no direct access to external objects but apprehends them only through ideas and data that are found in the mind.

Romanticism: In the arts and philosophy, the rejection of the view that "form" is most fundamental and that reason is most central to human life.

Self: That which one relates to as one's person, involving but not necessarily being exhausted by predominantly physical and psychological factors.

Socratic: Relating to the Greek philosopher Socrates or to his method of arriving at truth through asking questions and seeking definitions of concepts through critical conversation.

Spirit: A vital force in living beings. Though some identify this force in humans with the mind or with consciousness, others understand it more as a divine force or as something organic.

Stoic: An attitude arising from an ancient Greek school of philosophy that asserted that happiness can be achieved only by accepting life's ups and downs as the products of an unalterable fate.

Subjective (Hegel): That which is understood only as "inner" or as pertaining almost exclusively to the individual and not to a larger community or world.

Subjective Right (Hegel): The right to be free from interference. This right is important, but negative in the sense of not having specific content. It amounts to the opportunity to be left alone.

Sublimation: The channeling of impulses or energies often regarded as dangerous or unacceptable, especially sexual desires, toward activities regarded as more socially acceptable. The satisfactions coming from sublimation are often viewed as substitutes for what is really wanted.

Sublime: Of the highest esthetic or spiritual value and largely inaccessible to rational analysis.

Symbolism: The taking of some reality or realities to represent or give access to the meaning or nature of other realities.

Teleology: An approach that studies actions and things in relation to their ends, use, or purposes.

Terror: Intense or overwhelming fear; typically connected with threats to the very foundations of one's life upon which one has been able to trust and rely.

Theodicy: Arguments in defense of God's goodness in the face of what at least appears to be the existence of evil.

Totality: A bringing together of items that takes all relevant ones into account; these elements as so combined.

Transcendence: That which has an existence, place, or standing above, beyond, and apart from other things.

Transference: The process, especially in psychoanalysis or other psychotherapy, whereby feelings, fears, or emotions relevant to one domain or person are unwittingly redirected or repeated with regard to a new person or object, often the analyst or therapist.

Truth (Nietzsche): In Nietzsche, truth is defined as that which affirms life and promotes energy and growth. This type of affirmative power is the possession of rare individuals whom Nietzsche calls "supermen." (*Übermenschen*). More conventionally, truth is understood as a feature of propositions that accurately correspond to the reality.

Two-worldly: Belonging to this world as well as some other world beneath and/or beyond this one. Involves recognition of the fact that not all that is experienced and sought can be found in and explained by the elements present in this world.

Übergang: (German) Transition, usually a problematic and even perilous one.

Übermensch **(Nietzsche)**: (German) A superior kind of human being, especially in Nietzschean philosophy. Such beings are said to be able to overcome their prior conditions of being and, at the extreme, to overcome the limitations of humanity itself.

Uhrphenomenon **(Schopenhauer)**: (German) A special phenomenon, uniquely placed, that allows a person exceptional access to an underlying reality or to reality itself.

Unheimlichkeit **(Heidegger)**: (German) A sense of not being at home in the world.

Utopian: Having to do with an ideal or perfect state or place, usually viewed as unattainable.

Will: Executive part of one's being, through which decisions are made and actions are taken. Many controversies exist over whether this Will is free or determined by outside or hidden forces.

Wisdom: Often construed as involving, but also transcending knowledge and information and offering transformative guidance in living. The Ancients tended to believe that wisdom could be found, whereas the Moderns have tended to limit the basis for guidance in living to the realms of factual knowledge and information.

Zeitgeist: (German) The ideas prevalent in a particular historical period and place, especially as expressed in philosophy, religion, and the arts.

Biographical Notes

Alfred Adler (1870–1937). A Viennese physician, Adler was part of the early development of the psychoanalytic movement. Parting from Freud, Adler came to believe that the drive for power was our most fundamental motivator.

Ludwig von Beethoven (1770–1827). Major German composer of the Romantic period who was inspired by the French Revolution and its ideals. Among his famous symphonies are the *Eroica* and the *Ninth Symphony* (which includes Schiller's *Ode to Joy*). Becoming deaf at the early age of 32, Beethoven wrote his greatest music in his later life. When he died in 1827 in Vienna, more than 10,000 people streamed to the Austrian capital to attend his funeral. He had become a public figure as no composer had been before him, triumphing over personal tragedy. The artist as hero had been born.

Albert Camus (1913–1960). Algerian-born philosopher and writer who was greatly active in France during and after the Second World War. Camus is perhaps best known for his Existential novel, *The Stranger*. Camus is frequently connected with Sartre, though their views on the human predicament, and its resolution, differ. Camus won the Nobel Prize in Literature in 1957 and died in a car accident on his way to Paris in 1960.

René Descartes (1596–1650). Considered by most the father of modern philosophy (the period of the 17th and 18th centuries), Descartes was initially educated by Jesuits. He rejected a job in the church, however, for one in the army of Prince Maurice of Orange and Breda (Netherlands). Descartes resigned his commission in 1621 and moved to the Netherlands in 1628 to devote himself to his philosophy and a study of the physical theory of the universe, mathematics, and the examination of truth. He attempted to reconcile the claims of common sense with the developing concepts of the science generated by Galileo and others. He died in 1650 of pneumonia in Sweden, where he had gone several months earlier upon the invitation of the Swedish queen.

Friedrich Engels (1820–1895). The eldest son of a German industrialist, Engels was sent to London. He was so shocked by the working conditions in his father's factory that he joined the Communist League, which proclaimed "the overthrow of the bourgeoisie, the domination of the proletariat, the abolition of the old bourgeois society based on class antagonisms, and the establishment of a new society without classes and without private property." He met Karl Marx in London and financially supported Marx and his family. Together they wrote *The Communist Manifesto*, which was published in 1848.

Johann Fichte (1762–1814). A German philosopher, Fichte encountered Kant's philosophy when he was asked to tutor a student in Kant's theories. He became very concerned with extending and correcting the philosophy of the great Enlightenment thinker and had an unhappy meeting with Kant in 1791. Kant was not impressed. Fichte's *Addresses to the German Nation* (1808) is taken by many as a major step toward philosophical nationalism.

Michel Foucault (1926–1984). Perhaps the most famous and controversial French philosopher after Sartre, Foucault published widely on such topics as insanity, punishment, and sexuality. He attained the prestigious position of Chair in the History of Systems of Thought at the Collège de France and regularly lectured at the University of California at Berkeley.

Sigmund Freud (1856–1939). Born in Freiberg, Moravia (Austria), Freud spent most of his productive career as a physician and theorist in Vienna. His lectures and books about the conscious and the unconscious, and especially his theories about hysteria and sexual desires, brought him fame and following but also much controversy. After fleeing from the Nazis to London in 1939, he died of cancer a few months later. Freud is known as the father of psychoanalysis and first attained fame through the publication of the *Interpretation of Dreams*. Most of psychoanalytic thought remains in Freud's debt.

Johann Wolfgang von Goethe (1749–1832). The Shakespeare of the German world, Goethe wrote poetry and novels as well as reflections on science, particularly regarding color. Most major German philosophers saw Goethe as a prime example of creative talent and rational intellect. Goethe is most famous for his *Faust*, an epic drama written over a number of decades (1808, publication of part I). Living in Weimar, Goethe was also the advisor to those in political power.

Jürgen Habermas (1929–). A contemporary German philosopher, Habermas is concerned with political and social philosophy. Some would call him Neo-Marxist. He is especially concerned with examining communicative reason within a capitalist society, democracy, and the rule of law. His major work is *The Theory of Communicative Action* (1981). He is retired from teaching but remains an active writer and worldwide speaker.

Georg Wilhelm Friedrich Hegel (1770–1831). The most important of 19th-century German philosophers, Hegel was enthralled by the French Revolution and concerned with combining reason with history in order for history to be seen as a narrative of human development. In relative obscurity until after the publication of *The Phenomenology of Spirit* (1807), Hegel became a professor of philosophy at the University of Berlin and was viewed by many as a defender of the Prussian State in his later career.

Martin Heidegger (1889–1976). Author of *Being and Time* (1927), Heidegger became the major voice in German thought during the decades both prior to and after the Second World War. Because of his controversial connection with the Nazi Party, Heidegger became a very divisive figure in the world of political philosophy, and this fact made serious questioning of the relationship of philosophy, politics, and life unavoidable. Most of his career was lived out in the Black Forest region surrounding Freiburg, Germany, where he held the chair in philosophy at the university.

Johann Gottfried von Herder (1744–1803). Herder is one of the German "Romantic" philosophers who criticized Enlightenment thinking. He argued that a philosophy based on human reason alone, excluding human passions and desires, cannot be valid. For Herder, historical, cultural, and psychological factors have to be taken into consideration, and he opposed the idea of a reason-based philosophy that was timeless.

Edmund Husserl (1859–1938). Credited as the founder of the Phenomenological Movement, Husserl wrote extensively in the early decades of the 20th century regarding the task of philosophy, which he saw as description without assumptions or evaluations. Husserl held the chair in philosophy in Freiburg, Germany, prior to Heidegger and was of great influence on Heidegger's development of philosophical method.

Carl Gustav Jung (1875–1961). A noted researcher in his own right, Jung collaborated closely with Freud in the early stages of the development of the psychoanalytic movement. More sympathetic to religion and humanism in general than Freud, Jung came to believe that the quest for meaning was our most fundamental drive.

Immanuel Kant (1724–1804). Though he was born and spent virtually his entire life in Königsberg, Germany, Kant wrote the watershed work of modern Western philosophy, *The Critique of Pure Reason* (1781). Earlier in his career as a professor, Kant wrote important essays regarding the sciences and was highly respected throughout Europe. Later in his career, Kant attempted to reconcile free will and morality in their relation to deterministic claims made in science. His influence continues today.

Søren Kierkegaard (1813–1855). A Danish philosopher born in Copenhagen, Kierkegaard wrote voluminously during his short life, both on philosophical and religious topics. Viewed by some as a frivolous socialite, witty and superficial, Kierkegaard often wrote under pseudonyms. He attacked Hegelian philosophy and often under his own name cast scorn on the State Church of Denmark. Kierkegaard is called the "father of Existentialism."

Melanie Klein (1882–1960). An English psychoanalyst, Klein was central to the development of the object-relations school of psychoanalysis. She put great emphasis on the interpersonal as opposed to the standard Freudian claim that most all-important material is intrapsychic and thus internal to individuals. Freud's daughter, Anna, defended her father's views against what was labeled by many as the "Kleinian Heresy."

Karl Marx (1818–1883). Born in Germany, Marx lived out the bulk of his productive career in England. He was horrified by the working conditions in 19th-century England and contemptuous of the ways in which privilege was disguised by sophisticated theories. With Engels, his great friend and supporter, Marx wrote *The Communist Manifesto* (1848). The first volume of *Capital*, his major contribution to economic theory, was published in 1867. The later volumes were published posthumously by Engels.

John Stuart Mill (1806–1873). Educated from an early age by his father, James Mill, John Stuart Mill wrote works championing human liberty and the toleration of different ideas and lifestyles. Mill was a utilitarian concerned with promoting the greatest good for the greatest number of people. He made his living through employment in the office of the East India Company, where he became chief examiner of the India correspondence.

Wolfgang Amadeus Mozart (1756–1791). A major composer in the Western world, Mozart was born in Salzburg, Austria, and performed his music in many European courts from a very early age. He produced an astonishing volume of work in his short life. A number of philosophers, including Kierkegaard, considered Mozart's many compositions as the best that music had to offer and as examples of the highest realm of the aesthetic.

Friedrich Nietzsche (1844–1900). Born in Saxony, Nietzsche was educated in Bonn and Leipzig and became a professor of Classical Philology in Basel, Switzerland. Known by most as the trumpeter of the "Death of God," Nietzsche spent the last years of his sane life wandering among various boarding houses in Italy. Nietzsche had a famous friendship with Richard Wagner, the composer, and with him also a great falling out. Among Nietzsche's many works are *Thus Spake Zarathustra* and *Beyond Good and Evil*. Nietzsche went insane in 1889 and died in 1900.

Plato (427–347 B.C.). Perhaps the most influential philosopher in the West, Plato wrote dialogues regarding justice, love, law, politics, and the human soul. A young man at the time of Socrates's famous trial in Athens, Plato was enthralled by Socrates's method of inquiry. Going beyond Socrates, Plato developed metaphysical doctrines.

Jean-Jacques Rousseau (1712–1778). A French writer with interests ranging from education to the ordering of society, Rousseau greatly influenced those who are given credit (or blame) for the French Revolution. He is largely anti-intellectual and concerned more with emotion and authenticity. His *Discourse on the Arts and Sciences* (1750), *Emile* (1762), and *The Social Contract* (1762) ensured his fame and highly controversial status among almost all succeeding social thinkers.

Jean-Paul Sartre (1905–1980). A 20th-century French philosopher who was identified with the French resistance in World War II and made Existentialism popular as a movement, Sartre wrote novels, plays, and philosophical treatises such as *Being and Nothingness* (1943). After the Second World War, he became concerned with developing a political philosophy and had an extended flirtation with Marxist social and political ideas. Sartre was awarded the Nobel

Prize for literature in 1964, but he declined to accept the award to protest what he considered the degenerate values of bourgeois French society.

Arthur Schopenhauer (1788–1860). Known both as a pessimist and the philosopher who brought Buddhism to the attention of Western philosophy, Schopenhauer had very little in the way of a professional career. His major work, *The World as Will and Idea*, was published in 1818 but did not begin to receive attention until the 1850s. Schopenhauer is said by many to have influenced novelists such as Thomas Hardy, and the composer Richard Wagner claimed to be greatly in Schopenhauer's debt.

Socrates (469–399 B.C.). Viewed by many as the true originator of Western philosophy, Socrates wrote nothing but engaged fellow Athenians in conversations that challenged them to explain what they meant and knew. Partly because of political antagonisms in Athens, but also because of irritations stemming from his probing conversational inquiries, Socrates was arrested and charged with impiety and corruption of youth. Convicted, he was forced to drink hemlock.

Bibliography

Essential Reading:

Baynes, K., J. Bohman, and T. McCarthy, eds. *After Philosophy: End or Transformation?* Cambridge: MIT Press, 1989. This series of essays explores the limitations of philosophy and its possible future. The essays by Rorty, Foucault, Habermas, and MacIntyre may be particularly helpful. Many but not all of the 14 essays contain some difficult and technical material.

Beiser, Frederick. *The Fate of Reason: German Philosophy from Kant to Fichte.* Cambridge: Harvard University Press, 1987. This volume provides a helpful, though scholarly, rendering of a crucial period in the development of German Idealism. The accounts of Fichte and Schilling help to explain the genesis of Hegel's ideas.

Berlin, Isaiah. *Four Essays on Liberty.* Oxford: Oxford University Press, 1992. Berlin is a provocative and vivid writer, especially attuned to the history of ideas. His essay regarding different conceptions of liberty is lively and controversial.

———. *The Roots of Romanticism.* Edited by Henry Hardy. Princeton: Bollingen Press, 2001. Berlin may be at his best tracing those ideas and influences that led to various attacks on Enlightenment thinking and Rationalism more generally. As always, Berlin's scope is broad, and he can be read without a prior technical understanding of philosophical issues.

Bretall, Robert, ed. *A Kierkegaard Anthology.* Princeton: Princeton University Press, 1973. This collection of Kierkegaard's writings has carefully presented core portions of Kierkegaard's major works. It is best read sequentially, and the material from *Either/Or* is very well excerpted.

Camus, Albert. *The Plague.* Translated by Stuart Gilbert. New York: Vintage International, 1991. Viewed by many as a slightly disguised account of Nazi occupation, this novel poignantly conveys a pervasive kind of a human predicament and ways in which it can be confronted or often only endured.

———. *The Stranger.* Translated by Matthew Ward. New York: Vintage International, 1989. Probably Camus' best novel, *The Stranger* is both short and compelling. It should be noted that

Camus' diagnosis of human life is just one, but it may prove a good point of departure for understanding other Existential alternatives.

Erickson, Stephen. *The (Coming) Age of Thresholding.* Dordrecht, Netherlands: Kluwer Academic Publishers, 1999. This intriguing (but somewhat expensive and hard-to-find) book by your lecturer for this course addresses the future of philosophy and our present human predicament. Are we again, as in other spiritually precarious times, standing on the threshold of a new era?

Foucault, Michel. *Madness & Civilization, A History of Insanity in the Age of Reason.* Translated by Richard Howard. New York: Vintage Books, 1973. Many take this as Foucault's groundbreaking account of how power determines the structure of institutions and how accidents of circumstance may be crucial to how power works itself out. For those who wish to experience the flavor of Foucault's somewhat unusual style of writing, this may be the best work.

Freud, Sigmund. *The Interpretation of Dreams.* Translated by James Strachey. New York: Avon, 1980. This groundbreaking work firmly established Freud's reputation. Much of the early portions of this volume can be disregarded, for they involve his critical review and dismissal of alternative theories of dreaming and dreams.

―――. *Introductory Lectures on Psychoanalysis.* Translated by James Strachey and with a biographical introduction by Peter Gay. New York: W.W. Norton & Company, 1989. These lectures may be the best access to Freud for those who have never directly encountered his writing. Freud is usually far better than his commentators, and most of these lectures are altogether clear and lucid.

―――. *The Origins of Religion: Totem and Taboo, Moses and Monotheism, and Other Works.* Translated by James Strachey and edited by Albert Dickson. London: Penguin Books, 1985. These works by Freud are the central ones for understanding his largely negative attitudes toward religion. Freud is a gifted stylist and can be read relatively easily. There is little technical vocabulary and thus the works stand on their own. *Moses and Monotheism* may be the best place to start.

Fukuyama, Francis. *The End of History and the Last Man.* New York: Free Press, 1992. This engaging and highly provocative account looks at where history stood at the end of the Cold War. The last major section of the book considers Nietzsche's worry (more than 100 years ago) that we are heading toward a time of moral passivity and consumerism. Fukuyama writes well, and the section of this work involving Hegel is an enlightening read.

Gardner, Sebastian. *Routledge Philosophy Guidebook to Kant and the Critique of Pure Reason*. New York: Routledge, 1999. A clear overview of Kant's basic ideas as found in his *Critique of Pure Reason*, this work is largely accessible and conveys clearly and helpfully Kant's fundamental ideas.

Gay, Peter. *The Enlightenment: An Interpretation,* Volume II, *The Science of Freedom*. New York: W.W. Norton & Company, 1969. Gay provides a helpfully broad and culturally diverse account of the overall development of the issues that captivated and drove Enlightenment thinking.

Habermas, Jürgen. *The Philosophical Discourse of Modernity: Twelve Lectures*. Translated by Frederick Lawrence. Cambridge: MIT Press, 1990. This is a difficult book and is probably best considered only by those with a significant background in the history of European philosophy. These lectures may nonetheless be the best way to place Habermas within philosophical thought. This volume has greatly influenced a number of contemporary American philosophers.

Harvey, David. *The Condition of Postmodernity, An Enquiry into the Origins of Cultural Change*. Oxford: Basil Blackwell, 1989. Much controversy surrounds postmodernity, what it is, and whether we actually live in a postmodern period. Harvey's approach is both lucid and free of the tendentious.

Hegel, Georg Wilhelm Friedrich. *Elements of the Philosophy of Right*. Translated by H. Nisbet and edited by Allen Wood. Cambridge: Cambridge University Press, 1991. This is Hegel's basic work regarding the place and function of right in human morality and ethical life. The editor's introduction is quite helpful, as is the chronology provided of Hegel's writings and life.

Heidegger, Martin. *Being and Time*. Translated by John Macquarrie and Edward Robinson. New York: Harper & Row, 1962. This is Heidegger's major work. It lays out his lifelong project in forceful and intermittently clear ways. This work may be the most important philosophy text of the 20th century, though obviously this claim is much contested.

————.*An Introduction to Metaphysics.* Translated by Ralph Manheim. New Haven: Yale University Press, 1974. For many, this is Heidegger's most accessible work. Reflecting back on elements in Greek philosophy, Heidegger presents his own concerns with the meaning of life quite well. The first 20 pages or so are a helpful account of how Heidegger understands philosophy to function.

————. *The Question Concerning Technology and Other Essays.* Translated by William Lovitt. New York: Harper & Row, 1977. This volume contains Heidegger's central reflection on technology and its underlying place in our lives. Heidegger's important essay on the Nietzschean claim that "God is Dead" also appears here.

Jones, W. T. *The Romantic Syndrome: Toward a New Method in Cultural Anthropology and History of Ideas.* Dordrecht, Netherlands: Kluwer Academic Publishers, 2002. Jones provides criteria by which what is varyingly referred to as the "Romantic" can be better understood and evaluated. Quite readable, this book is underappreciated and quite insightful.

Jung, C. G. *Modern Man in Search of a Soul.* Translated by W. Dell and Cary Baynes. New York: A Harvest Book, Harcourt Brace Jovanovich, first published in 1933. This is a quite readable set of reflections by Jung on our human predicament as contemporary people. Jung is often somewhat diffuse, but in these writings he blends psychological and spiritual reflections in a largely concise way.

Kant, Immanuel. *Religion within the Limits of Reason Alone.* Translated by Theodore M. Greene and Hoyt H. Hudson. New York: Harper and Row, 1960. This is Kant's central and most exhaustive work regarding the relation of reason and religion and the hopes for religion that Kant thought to be plausible after the Enlightenment.

Kaufmann, Walter. *Hegel.* New York: Doubleday, 1965. Kaufmann's book is both insightful and at the same time chatty. In the context of developments in German culture and ideas regarding art and human life, he places Hegel in the broader European cultural scene.

Kierkegaard, Søren. *Either/Or, Part I.* Translated by Howard Hong and Edna Hong. Princeton: Princeton University Press, 1987. Here Kierkegaard provides an account of the kind of life he believes most people to live and few people to escape. Reflections are provided regarding music, seduction, and calculations of enjoyment. The most literary portion is at the end of this volume, *The Diary of a Seducer*, and is Kierkegaard at his best.

————. *Papers and Journals: A Selection*. Translated by Alastair Hannay. London: Penguin Books, 1996. These variegated Kierkegaardian writings, most not meant for publication, offer diverse insights and an appreciation of the relation of Kierkegaard's thinking to his own life. This is a good book for browsing.

Kohut, Heinz. *How Does Analysis Cure?* Edited by Arnold Goldberg. Chicago: University of Chicago Press, 1984. An important work in the field of therapeutic practice, this book conveys one of the major alternatives to a traditional approach to psychoanalytic interpretation. Many claim Kohut to be the major alternative to Freud in our time, and this is a good place to capture much of the core of his thinking.

Lowrie, Walter. *A Short Life of Kierkegaard*. Princeton: Princeton University Press, 1958. For those wishing a very brief account of Kierkegaard, the person, and the life he lived in Copenhagen, this book is quite clear and enjoyable.

Magee, Bryan. *The Philosophy of Schopenhauer*. Oxford: Clarendon Press (Oxford University Press), 1997. Magee is an especially clear and engaging writer who presents Schopenhauer in a comprehensive way, but one that also brings very clearly into focus Schopenhauer's understanding of the human predicament and consequent pessimism.

Marcuse, Herbert. *Reason and Revolution: Hegel and the Rise of Social Theory*. New York: Humanities Press, 1963. A guru to many during the 1960s, Marcuse provides provocative ideas regarding the transition from reason to social criticism in the development of philosophical thought. The account of Hegel slants somewhat in a Marxist direction.

Marx, Karl. *The Marx-Engels Reader*. Edited by Robert Tucker. New York: W.W. Norton & Company, 1972. This is one of the better compilations of classical Marxist writings. Most of the core ideas can be found in this book. The selections may be read out of sequence.

————. *Writings of the Young Marx on Philosophy and Society*. Translated and edited by L. Easton and K. Guddat. New York: Anchor Books, 1967. Many make a distinction between an exploratory and plausibly critical Marx and a later, dogmatic and doctrinaire Marx. In this book, many of the elements that characterize the early Marx are found.

Nehamas, Alexander. *Nietzsche, Life as Literature.* Cambridge: Harvard University Press, 1985. This is perhaps the best study of Nietzsche that brings the analytic sophistication of American philosophy to bear. Nehamas is a lucid writer who keeps Nietzsche's driving ideas in the center of his discussion.

Nietzsche, Friedrich. *Beyond Good and Evil.* Translated by Walter Kaufmann. New York: Vintage Books, 1966. Many claim that this work is the best entry to Nietzsche's thinking. Written sometimes in brief aphorisms and other times in much longer sections, *Beyond Good and Evil* allows a measure of browsing.

———. *On the Genealogy of Morals* (and) *Ecce Homo.* Translated by Walter Kaufmann. New York: Vintage Books, 1969. *The Genealogy of Morals* provides Nietzsche's best account of how our moral life originated and how conceptions of the Good made their earliest historical appearances. *Ecce Homo* is a startling and fascinating work written in the year directly before Nietzsche went mad.

———. *The Portable Nietzsche.* Edited by Walter Kaufman. New York: Viking Press, 1968. This remains perhaps the best collection of various portions of Nietzsche's major writings. Nietzsche's most poetic work, *Thus Spake Zarathustra,* is included in its totality and provides literary access to many of Nietzsche's ideas.

Ott, Hugo. *Martin Heidegger, A Political Life.* Translated by Allan Blunden. London: BasicBooks (HarperCollins), 1993. More than any other work, this book clearly and unambiguously presents the history of Heidegger's involvement with the Nazi Party. Ott writes primarily as a biographer, and an understanding of Heidegger's philosophy is not necessary for comprehending the basic narrative of Heidegger's political involvements.

Pinkard, Terry. *Hegel's Phenomenology: The Sociality of Reason,* New York: Cambridge University Press, 1994. Pinkard is one of the better and more lucid expositors of Hegel's philosophy and particularly of the way in which Hegel makes reason a more social phenomenon than did his predecessors.

Postman, Neil. *Technopoly: The Surrender of Culture to Technology.* New York: Vintage Books, 1993. This is a highly readable account of how technology both helps and can hinder us, how it involves "winners" and "losers," and how an ever-growing technological civilization involves dangers to our imaginative selves.

Reppen, J., ed. *Beyond Freud, A Study of Modern Psychoanalytic Theorists.* Hillsdale, NJ: The Analytic Press, 1985. This is a set of 14 probing and largely accessible essays regarding a variety of psychoanalytic practitioners and theorists reflecting on the status and future of psychoanalysis. The essays concerning Bowlby, Gill, Mahler, Kohut, and Grünbaum are of special interest.

Sartre, Jean-Paul. *Being and Nothingness, An Essay on Phenomenological Ontology.* Translated and with an introduction by Hazel Barnes. New York: Washington Square Press, 1993. This is Sartre's major philosophical work and the one that firmly established his philosophical reputation. To the degree that anyone wants direct contact with Sartre's fundamental philosophy, this is the place to find it. It is, however, a challenging book.

———. *Nausea.* Translated by Lloyd Alexander. New York: New Directions, 1969. This novel conveys in vivid ways the sense that there may be no meaning to be found in the world around us. It is a short novel and a good alternative for those who do not want to undertake a reading of Sartre's philosophical prose.

Schopenhauer, Arthur. *The Will to Live.* Edited by Richard Taylor. New York: Ungar, 1967. This is a collection of Schopenhauer's core writings as well as a helpful, short timeline of Schopenhauer's life. These writings are an economical way of reading Schopenhauer himself and of coming to appreciate his graceful and provocative style.

Taylor, Charles. *Sources of the Self: The Making of the Modern Identity.* Cambridge: Harvard University Press, 1989. This book gives a well-written overview of how our contemporary sense of ourselves has been influenced by various elements in the history of philosophy. The account of various aspects of Romanticism is particularly helpful.

Tucker, Robert. *Philosophy and Myth in Karl Marx.* Cambridge: Cambridge University Press, 1964. This is a helpful overview of Marx, what he said and did not say. Tucker casts a wide net and catches numerous connections between Marx and those who either influenced him or were influenced by him.

Wolin, Richard, ed. *The Heidegger Controversy: A Critical Reader.* Cambridge: MIT Press, 1993. An excellent set of diverse and conflicting interpretations of Heidegger's politics and his philosophical thought. Those wishing to grasp the core of the political controversies regarding Heidegger are usefully directed to this volume.

Supplementary Reading:

Arendt, Hannah. *The Human Condition*. Chicago: University of Chicago Press, 1998. Arendt writes immensely well and is most concerned with reflecting on various aspects of the human situation in our time. Her work combines sophistication with direct appeal to vital issues about which any thoughtful person will be concerned.

Berlin, Isaiah. *The Crooked Timber of Humanity*. Princeton: Princeton University Press, 1990. These essays are helpful in mapping historical movements such as Romanticism. Berlin is more generally concerned with mapping various reactions to Rationalism. His essays are interrelated and to some extent overlap but can be read to advantage separately.

Brée, Germaine. *Camus and Sartre, Crisis and Commitment*. New York: Dell Publishing, 1972. Educated both in Europe and in the United States, Brée provides a valuable backdrop for understanding the development of French Existentialism. She is quite good at conveying both the commonalities and the divergences between Sartre and Camus.

Cate, Curtis. *Friedrich Nietzsche*. New York: The Overlook Press, 2005. This work is an extensive and detailed biography of Nietzsche's life, with continuing reference to Nietzsche's thought. Cate is strongest in his provision of historical data. Some of the inferences that he draws are controversial for Nietzsche scholars.

Engell, James. *The Creative Imagination: Enlightenment to Romanticism*. Cambridge: Harvard University Press, 1981. This is a careful account of both relations and tensions between human reason and the development of the notion of imagination in cultural thought in Europe.

Fischer, Ernst. *The Necessity of Art: A Marxist Approach*. Translated by Anna Bostock. New York: Penguin Books, 1978. Fischer, though himself a Marxist, looks beyond economic dogmas and presents an engaging if flawed account of culture as seen from a Marxist perspective. It has often been hard for many to find Marxism at all plausible. Fischer may not succeed, but he breeds life into the Marxist perspective.

Fromm, Eric. *Marx's Concept of Man*, and an excerpt (translated by T. B. Bottomore) from *Marx's Economic and Philosophical Manuscripts*. New York: Frederick Ungar Publishing, 1973. Fromm is accused by many of being merely a popularizer. Though this accusation may be fair, Fromm is nonetheless direct and makes Marxian ideas directly relevant to our understanding of the human situation. The excerpts from Marx's writing are well chosen.

Fukuyama, Francis. *Our Posthuman Future, Consequences of the Biotechnology Revolution*. New York: Farrar, Straus and Giroux, 2002. Fukuyama writes well and is prepared to take on large and largely unmanageable problems. In this work, he considers the implications of advances in medicine and biotechnology as the 21st century progresses.

Garff, Joakim. *Søren Kierkegaard: A Biography*. Translated by Bruce Kirmmse. Princeton: Princeton University Press, 2005. Recently published, this is the most extensive biography of Kierkegaard's life now available in English. It provides a clear account of the crises that drove Kierkegaard's philosophy. There may be more detail in this book than some readers wish to absorb.

Gay, Peter. *Freud, A Life for Our Time*. New York: Anchor Books (Doubleday), 1989. Gay blends historical and cultural information in a way that sheds very useful light on Freud, the person, and Freud, the thinker. Free of jargon, this work will be of special interest to those who enjoy cultural history.

Gray, John. *Berlin*. London: Fontana Press, 1995. Perhaps the best account of Isaiah Berlin's thinking regarding the plurality of human values and the place of liberty in their midst. Gray is able to convey important aspects of many of today's controversies in political philosophy.

Guignon, C. and D. Pereboom, eds. *Existentialism, Basic Writings*. Indianapolis: Hackett, 1995. Major representatives of Existential philosophy and its concern with personal existence are anthologized in this book. Any of the writers represented can be read separately from the others.

Habermas, Jürgen. *Moral Consciousness and Communicative Action*. Translated by C. Lenhardt and S.W. Nicholsen. Cambridge: MIT Press, 2001. For Habermas, communication has moral obligations and emancipatory potential. He is very concerned with championing democratic values and rational community. This work conveys much of the spirit and strategies of Habermas's thought.

Hegel, Georg Wilhelm Friedrich. *Phenomenology of Spirit.* Translated by A.V. Miller. Oxford: Oxford University Press, 1977. This is Hegel's groundbreaking work that brought him to prominence. In it, he places himself in relation to his predecessors and provides an account of the unfolding of the human spirit. Though challenging, the preface provides a dramatic overview of Hegel's thought.

Heidegger, Martin. *Basic Writings.* Edited by David Farrell Krell. New York: Harper & Row, 1977. This is perhaps the best compilation of Heidegger's core writings. The *Letter on Humanism* is Heidegger's attempt to distance himself from Existentialism in general and what he thinks of as merely humanistic thinking. Readers should be warned that many find Heidegger's writing an acquired taste.

Kant, Immanuel. *Critique of Pure Reason.* Translated by N. K. Smith. London: Macmillan Press, 1964. Kant's watershed work is extremely difficult to read, but this is the bone on which philosophers have gnawed ever since it first appeared. Probably the prefaces and the introduction are most accessible. The *Critique* discusses the function and limits of human reason.

————. *Groundwork of the Metaphysics of Morals.* Translated by H. J. Paton. New York: Harper & Row, 1964. An important and more accessible writing of Kant that stresses basic elements with respect to moral life as Kant himself understands it.

Kierkegaard, Søren. *Either/Or, Part II.* Translated by Howard Hong and Edna Hong. Princeton: Princeton University Press, 1987. These writings, presented as letters of admonition and instruction to those who live the aesthetic life described in *Either/Or, Part I,* are especially revealing regarding Kierkegaard's notions of commitment and responsibility.

Klein, Melanie. *The Psycho-Analysis of Children.* Translated by Alix Strachey. New York: Dell Publishers, 1975. Klein represents a divergence from classical Freudianism and is claimed by many to be the first important originator of views that are Freudian yet differ from his specific ideas. Klein is not a smooth read, but her ideas are important, and this volume provides much of their core.

Lévi, Bernard-Henri. *Sartre: The Philosopher of the Twentieth Century*. Translated by Andrew Brown. Cambridge, UK: Polity Press, 2003. An author who provokes strong negative or positive reactions, Lévi attempts a serious account of Sartre and his influences. Readers will learn quickly whether this book is right for them. It is relatively free of jargon and is an engaging work.

Löwith, Karl. *From Hegel to Nietzsche: The Revolution in Nineteenth-Century Thought*. Translated by David Green. New York: Anchor Books, 1967. Read by many who seek an understanding of the transformation in thinking among philosophers in Europe from an emphasis on "Thought" to an emphasis on "Will." This book may be more helpful to those already acquainted with European philosophy.

————. *Martin Heidegger and European Nihilism*. Translated by Gary Steiner. New York: Columbia University Press, 1995. This is a sharply outlined pursuit of the relation between Heidegger and various political and nihilistic developments that are occurring around him. The political dimensions of Heidegger's work receive special attention.

Magee, Bryan. *Wagner and Philosophy*. London: Penguin Press, 2000. Magee's work is of enormous cultural value. It provides an insightful and sweeping account of the influence of Schopenhauer on Wagner and Nietzsche and also of the complicated and important relationship between Wagner and Nietzsche. *Wagner and Philosophy* is entertaining reading, though a few of its sections are slightly demanding. It is also published in the United States under the title, *The Tristan Chord*.

Malcolm, Janet. *Psychoanalysis: The Impossible Profession*. New York: Vintage Books, 1982. This is an account of the way work was done within the psychoanalytic community in New York only a few decades ago. Malcolm's interviews and reflections offer both gossipy information and clear accounts of the controversies surrounding psychoanalytic methods of treatment.

Matustík, M. and M. Westphal, eds. *Kierkegaard in Post-Modernity*. Bloomington: Indiana University Press, 1995. This collection of essays works to sort out the relation among Existentialists and between classic Existential thinkers and the world in which they found themselves. The table of contents offers the reader clear choices regarding which particular thinkers to consider. The essays are quite separable from each other.

May, R. *Love and Will*. New York: Dell Publishing, 1969. May has the gift of making issues in depth psychology clear and engaging. No jargon is involved. Though some slight background in Existential philosophy would be helpful, this work can stand on its own.

May, R., E. Angel, and H. Ellenberger, eds. *Existence: A New Dimension in Psychiatry and Psychology*. New York: Basic Books, 1958. The anthologized articles in this collection do a thoughtful job of relating psychotherapy to Existential thinking. The introductory essays by May and Ellenberger provide excellent overviews of this area. Also contained is a famous case conveyed by Ludwig Binswanger, *viz.*, *The Case of Ellen West*. Mysterious and not altogether accessible, this presentation is one of the most intriguing reflections on whether suicide is ever an appropriate life decision.

Merquior, J. G. *Foucault*. Berkeley: University of California Press, 1985. In a short, quite lucid account of Foucault, Merquior stresses his ideas more than his life. This is perhaps the best concise introduction to Foucault, the thinker.

Miller, James. *The Passion of Michel Foucault*. New York: Simon & Schuster, 1993. Perhaps the best account of the life of Foucault and his importance in both postwar France and the United States. Miller conveys Foucault's ideas and their motivations almost effortlessly, and the work itself helps to make plausible how philosophy might directly connect with life.

Philipse, Herman. *Heidegger's Philosophy of Being: A Critical Interpretation*. Princeton: Princeton University Press, 1998. Philipse writes a careful, clearly developed account of what Heidegger seeks in his quest to discover the meaning of being. Also contained is an excellent account of those who have influenced Heidegger's work.

Pippin, Robert. *Hegel's Idealism: The Satisfactions of Self-Consciousness*. New York: Cambridge University Press, 1989. This is a core exposition of Hegel's understanding of the relation of reason to reality and human consciousness. Pippin is demanding but casts very helpful light on Hegel's place in the history of ideas in the early 19th century.

Rosen, Stanley. *Nihilism, A Philosophical Essay*. South Bend, IN: St. Augustine's Press, 2000. Nihilism has meant different things to different writers. Rosen is an energetic thinker who works to defend foundations, both traditional and metaphysical, from what many perceive as the fashionable corrosive tendencies displayed by nihilistic thinkers.

Safranski, Rüdiger. *Martin Heidegger, Between Good and Evil.* Translated by Ewald Osers. Cambridge: Harvard University Press, 1998. Extremely well written and also of high literary merit, this work provides a vivid impression both of Heidegger the thinker and Heidegger as a person in the world. Many claim this is the best and also the least biased account of Heidegger's intellectual life.

————. *Nietzsche: A Philosophical Biography.* Translated by Shelly Frisch. New York: W.W. Norton & Company, 2003. Safranski captures the temperament, phases, and moods of Nietzsche's thinking extraordinarily well. Though it is useful already to know some of the history of 19th-century European ideas, Safranski offers a most helpful first approach to Nietzsche in any case.

————. *Schopenhauer and the Wild Years of Philosophy.* Translated by Ewald Osers. Cambridge: Harvard University Press, 1987. Safranski is always an engaging read, combining literary and philosophical ideas with considerable grace. Some may find that a prior understanding of German thought and philosophy is most helpful before this work is undertaken.

Sartre, Jean-Paul. *No Exit and Three Other Plays.* Translated by Stuart Gilbert. New York: Vintage, 1989. For those whose orientation is dramatic, these plays provide vivid and stark accounts of Sartre's Existentialism. If only one play is read, it should probably be *No Exit.*

Shamdasani, S. and M. Münchow, eds. *Speculations After Freud: Psychoanalysis, Philosophy and Culture.* New York: Routledge, 1994. This is a collection of reflections on the relation of psychoanalytic theory to culture as well as some ruminations on the future of psychoanalysis as a potential contributor to cultural analyses. The articles by Kristeva, Richardson, and Scott are of especial interest.

Strawson, P. F. *The Bounds of Sense, An Essay on Kant's Critique of Pure Reason.* London: Methuen & Co., 1966. Strawson's influential book presents Kant's fundamental concepts and their connection to each other. Though demanding, Strawson's writing is insightful and provides an opportunity to observe a professional philosopher at work with difficult concepts.

Tarnas, Richard. *The Passion of the Western Mind*. New York: Ballantine Books, 1993. Tarnas provides a highly readable adventure through the history of Western philosophical thinking. More than most, Tarnas relates what are often technical dimensions of philosophy to real issues in human life.

Wicks, Robert. *Modern French Philosophy, From Existentialism to Postmodernism*. Oxford: Oneworld, 2003. In this volume, a very helpful overview is provided of 20th-century French philosophy and the setting in which it emerged. Many writers are discussed who had striking and controversial beliefs regarding the problems of human existence.

Wolin, Richard. *The Seduction of Unreason: The Intellectual Romance with Fascism, from Nietzsche to Postmodernism*. Princeton: Princeton University Press, 2004. Wolin is gifted and writes clearly. There have been numerous reactions to an alleged suffocation of society, culture, and the individual through an excessive reliance on the mechanisms of rationality. Many of these reactions come from the right side of the political spectrum. This is a useful book for exploring these reactions and what motivates them.

Yalom, Irvin. *Love's Executioner and Other Tales of Psychotherapy*. New York: Basic Books, 1989. A set of reflections based on case material, Yalom's work brings to life what the actual practice of psychotherapy is like. His particular concern in these essays is the resolution of transferences, those ways in which ghosts from our past haunt our present.

———. *The Schopenhauer Cure*. New York: HarperCollins, 2005. Himself a practicing psychoanalyst, Yalom is able to present Schopenhauer's remedies for human suffering in a vivid way. This novel is an excellent first read for those who would like to have Schopenhauer's understanding of human existence brought to life. Because much of Yalom's interest has to do with therapy itself, this work is a good bridge to a number of post-Freudian ideas.

———. *When Nietzsche Wept*. New York: HarperCollins, 1993. This novel is largely fictional with respect to its factual information but very insightful in bringing Nietzsche, the person, and his therapeutic ideas to life.

Yankelovich, Daniel and William Barrett. *Ego and Instinct, The Psychoanalytic View of Human Nature—Revised*. New York: Random House, 1970. This is an important and also much undervalued contextualization of large issues regarding the status and future of the enterprise of psychoanalytic practice and theory. The first chapter is well worth reading in its own right.

Internet Resources:

"Major Figures in Western Philosophy," *Philosophy Pages,* http://www.philosophypages.com/ph/. A helpful website that provides an introduction to the major figures in Western philosophy and gives links to their most important writings.

"A Collated Web Index of Significant Historians and Philosophers," *Scholiast.org, Margin Notes for the World Wide Web,* www.scholiast.org/history/histphil.html. This Web site provides an overview of the history of philosophy from the Classical Period through the Modern Period.